# MAMA'S
# BIG BOOK
## *of* LITTLE LIFESAVERS

# MAMA'S BIG BOOK

## of LITTLE LIFESAVERS

**398** WAYS TO SAVE YOUR TIME, MONEY, AND SANITY

by *Kerry Colburn*

**CHRONICLE BOOKS**

SAN FRANCISCO

Library of Congress Cataloging-in-Publication Data:
Colburn, Kerry.
Mama's big book of little lifesavers : 398 ways to save your time,
money, and sanity / by Kerry Colburn.
        p. cm.
    ISBN 978-0-8118-7864-7
    1. Child rearing. 2. Parenting.  I. Title.
    HQ769.C63176 2011
    649'.1—dc22

                              2010030876


Manufactured in China.
Designed by Jennifer Tolo Pierce

10 9 8 7 6 5 4 3 2 1

Chronicle Books LLC
680 Second Street
San Francisco, California 94107
www.chroniclebooks.com

# CONTENTS

# INTRODUCTION

$A$s a parent, you very quickly become an expert in day-to-day family survival—because from the moment your beautiful baby is born, it's sink or swim time. It's up to you to learn how to get through each day with your child reasonably taken care of and your own wits (and hopefully your sense of humor) reasonably intact. And so you do. You unravel the mystery of how to move your sleeping infant from car seat to crib, high-five yourself when you remember a spare outfit in the diaper bag, and call your mom friends to celebrate your first successful babysitter drop-off. You learn new essential skills such as how

to salvage a favorite action figure from the toilet, negotiate a meeting without revealing the spit-up on your back, and keep your eyes open during date night. You are awesome!

Without even really realizing it, every day you are succeeding in dozens of small but significant ways. And along the way, you are filling your own personal parenting toolbox with what works for you: a trick here, a bribe there, a funny song that diffuses a battle, a seemingly insignificant technique that helps you navigate the hours from wake-up to bedtime over and over again. You, my friend, are becoming a parenting pro. But as you've certainly learned by now, even a pro can use a little backup—especially when new surprises crop up that you never saw coming.

The years from birth until your kids enter grade school is a wondrous, challenging, and eye-opening period, full of change, discoveries, and major peaks and valleys. This is arguably the time you log the most active and strenuous parenting hours of your career—and the time you need all the help you can get. Wouldn't it be a beautiful thing if other parents' toolboxes were open for you to paw through and test out? Alas, it's not always that easy. Moms and dads simply don't share their insider tricks with one another with any kind of consistency or frequency. There are several possible reasons for this: They're tired. They do what they do so unconsciously they might not even

remember that it was once a hard-won technique. They are so enmeshed in their own quirky systems that they forget to ask what works for someone else.

Sure, everyone asks for advice on big things such as discipline and potty training and sleep. But what about the myriad little techniques that help smooth over the bulk of each day? If only you could be a fly on the wall at other parents' houses, you'd learn a lot of good stuff. And it sure would be a lot faster than figuring it all out on your own.

Let *Mama's Big Book of Little Lifesavers* do this for you. Inside this book you'll find hundreds of ways to save time, money, and your sanity—culled from my own experience and that of parents of young children from coast to coast. Parents of all types generously contributed their big and small secrets for success, in hopes of helping their compatriots: city parents, suburban parents, parents of multiples, single parents, and even a few grandparents. (Happily, this meant I learned a lot of new tricks, too.) There's a reason for the old adage that "it takes a village to raise a child." Parenting is a team sport. Don't try to figure everything out on your own. Instead, raise the white flag (a clean diaper will do nicely) and tap out your SOS—other parents will *always* come to your rescue. And let this book be your handy personal flotation device to cling to. Hey, it just might buoy you up to face another day.

Good luck to you, fellow parent! I salute you.

—Kerry

# HOW TO USE THIS BOOK

*Mama's Big Book of Little Lifesavers* is organized into three main sections: **TIME-SAVERS, MONEY-SAVERS,** and **SANITY-SAVERS.** The content within each section is loosely organized from babyhood through kindergarten. The book is meant to dip in and out of, whenever you need a little pick-me-up or some fresh inspiration on navigating life with kids. (After all, who has time to read chapters?) Flip through it and see what catches your fancy or speaks to a challenge you're struggling with this week. Share the ideas with your friends. For times when you need help on a specific subject—say, toothbrushing or airplane travel—refer to the Quick Help Guide that follows.

# QUICK HELP GUIDE

While you'll find dozens of tips on these subjects and more throughout the book, here's a handy way to get started if you've got a specific challenge *right now*.

• • • ━━ ━━ ━━ • • •

**BATHING AND BRUSHING**
*Tips:* 3, 18, 30, 43, 95, 159, 263, 302, 311, 328

**BED- AND NAPTIME**
*Tips:* 29, 33, 36, 117, 133, 257, 259, 260, 270, 372

**BIRTHDAYS AND HOLIDAYS**
*Tips:* 85, 87, 153, 172, 181, 184, 188, 246, 256, 336

**DIAPERS AND THE POTTY**
*Tips:* 1, 38, 52, 138, 156, 158, 160, 170, 192, 331

**BEHAVIOR AND BRIBES**
*Tips:* 55, 61, 220, 245, 302, 334, 335, 336, 359, 391

**GETTING DRESSED AND OUT THE DOOR**
*Tips:* 12, 41, 54, 63, 68, 80, 81, 101, 108, 120, 358

**HOUSEHOLD CHALLENGES**
*Tips:* 4, 7, 91, 105, 109, 121, 235, 236, 300, 304

**MEALS AND SNACKS**
*Tips:* 23, 31, 39, 44, 48, 78, 116, 177, 278, 349, 376

**TRAVEL SURVIVAL**
*Tips:* 21, 37, 46, 114, 163, 293, 297, 375

**YOU AND YOUR PARTNER**
*Tips:* 24, 59, 118, 255, 301, 303, 346, 353, 398

TIME-SAVERS

Time becomes an even more precious commodity when you're a parent. Not only will you always long for just a little more time for yourself—to sleep, to read, perchance to shower—you will also crave more time to simply enjoy your children. What parents need are simple, easy-to-employ efficiencies that can save a few minutes here, a few minutes there, and lots of irritation all around. After all, no one likes to feel rushed, and nothing slows down kids (or frankly, adults) more than yelling, "Hurry! We're late *again*!"

My hope is that these time-savers will do just what you need: help you cut down some valuable time that's spent on annoyances or drudgery (getting shoes on, doing laundry, putting toys away, etc.) and leave you with just a little more cushion for fun. After all, if you can make yourself even fifteen minutes more efficient tomorrow morning, that's fifteen more minutes to tickle your baby, chase your naked toddler, dance around the living room with your preschoolers . . . or just finish your cup of coffee while it's still hot. Dream big!

**1** Save time (and your back) by not trudging upstairs or to the other end of the house for every diaper change, for Pete's sake! Throw a towel on the couch, floor, or ottoman, and save yourself several thousand trips. Keep small baskets of diapering supplies in different spots in your home, too, for further efficiency.

**2** If you're bottle-feeding, resist automatically warming up the bottles. Instead, take your premade bottles straight out of the fridge (or mix your dry formula with unheated water). If baby accepts bottles either cold or at room temperature from the get-go, you save yourself time, effort, and future headaches—especially when you're out or traveling.

**3** A sponge bath—or simply dunking baby's bottom into the sink when needed—saves time, water, and mess, and it's better for baby's skin anyway. Even older kids do not need a bath every day; consider a hands-and-face wash (or hands-face-feet in summertime) as part of the bedtime routine instead. You'll not only save tub time, but cleanup and laundry time as well.

- - - ▬ ▬ ▬ - - -

**4** Take a cue from busy hotel housekeepers and keep extra garbage bags and/or diaper-pail liners at the bottom of the pail, so you can replace easily when you take out the trash.

- - - ▬ ▬ ▬ - - -

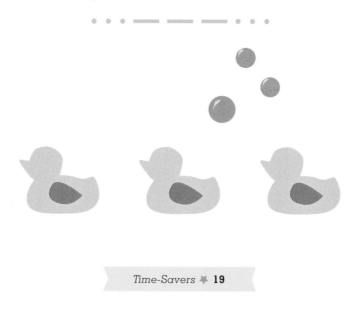

**5**

"On my shopping trips before she was born, I bought extra of everything we normally would run out of, such as toothpaste, detergent, toilet paper, contact lens solution . . . things that you might have to make a quick stop at the store for, but that isn't as easy to do with a newborn." —*Jennifer*

**6** If you're bottle-feeding at night, keep pre-measured formula and a bottle of water on your nightstand to save a trip to the kitchen—especially if it's on another floor. If you're using breast milk, remember it keeps at room temperature for up to eight hours, so if you're nodding off at 10 p.m. and baby will be eating at 2 a.m., you can just set it on your nightstand. If feedings are farther apart (or not that predictable), keep the bottle and an ice pack in a portable cooler, insulated lunch bag, or dorm fridge, ready to go.

**7** If you live on two floors, keep a handled basket or reusable shopping bag at the top and bottom of the staircase, to transport all the things you need to go up or down (stack of diapers, bottles, blankie, toilet paper, your own water bottle, book, etc.). As kids get older, the system still works—and they can help—by using the bag to cart toys, jackets, books, and more.

• • • ▬ ▬ ▬ • • •

**8** A good telephone headset means you don't have to wait for nap time to make your personal or work phone calls. Put baby in carrier of choice and walk or bounce on an exercise ball while making hands-free calls—you get some exercise and the baby enjoys the sound of your voice, so you might as well use it. A headset will also allow you to multitask while breast-feeding or pumping.

• • • ▬ ▬ ▬ • • •

**9**

"I use my time pumping as my personal hygiene time: flossing, brushing teeth, taking vitamins, putting on under-eye concealer, plucking eyebrows. A hands-free bra is essential for this." —*Christina*

**10** Keep a good selection of food-delivery menus right next to your phone, with favorite dishes circled, for quick meal solutions when your energy is low.

**11** Instead of pumping into those special bottles that come with your breast pump and then transferring the milk to freezer bags, pump right into a bag by attaching it with a rubber band. You save transfer time, bottle-washing and drying time, *and* avoid any chance of spillage—which will take even more time to replace.

**12** Keep a pre-packed diaper bag (or what you're using as a diaper bag) near the front door so you can get out of the house more quickly. The less time it takes you to get organized, the more likely you are to follow through on planned outings.

· · · ━━ ━━ ━━ · · ·

**13** Have everything you can think of delivered, and save yourself not only shopping time, but the time it takes to get yourself and baby dressed and out the door. When your new baby is sleeping, register for several delivery services that will be helpful in the coming months: meals, diapers, groceries, organic produce, drugstore items, etc. Once you have online accounts and basic shopping lists set up, it will be a breeze to get your shopping done—just click to reorder—and many sites offer free delivery, too.

· · · ━━ ━━ ━━ · · ·

**14**

"Diapers.com—I love this service for recurring and bulky things such as diapers, formula, wipes, etc. They have free next-day shipping for any big orders. If I see that formula is low in the morning, the next day I have it delivered at the door. So convenient." —*Aya*

**15** Learn to side-lie nurse early. That way you can catch some valuable snooze time while baby nurses at night.

**16** Save yourself a ton of cooking and cleanup time by following this simple rule: Anyone who wants to come and visit the baby has to bring a meal for the whole family.

**17** When your baby is young, your house can feel out of order, and it becomes a chore to hunt down simple things. Keep a handled basket or tray of the kinds of items you always want nearby but can't always get up to retrieve: cell or cordless phone, TV remote control, extra pacifier, burp cloth, lip balm, water bottle. Move the basket when you move.

• • • ━━ ━━ ━━ • • •

**18** Bathe baby and yourself at the same time. It's an efficient solution when you realize no one has cleaned themselves in three days—and it can be a great ritual for working parents to get some quality time with baby after a long day away.

• • • ━━ ━━ ━━ • • •

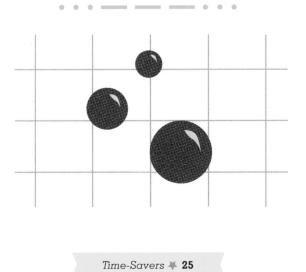

# 19. Baby Book?
# What Baby Book?

Who has time to print out photos, identify them all, and paste them into a lovely scrapbook? Sure, you'll do it someday . . . in the meantime, try these quicker baby book alternatives:

 Jot down simple notes about your baby in a blank notebook that you keep handy in the living room or in your bag.

 Set up an e-mail account for your child and send him quick notes about what's happening in his life and how you're feeling watching him grow. You can also attach pictures.

 Set aside a box or drawer in which to toss things such as baby cards, well-baby doctor reports, and keepsakes.

 Create an online album on one of the many photo Web sites, where you can just dump picures from your camera or phone and alert friends and family where to find them.

"Google's Picasa is my time-saver and demanding grandparents' delight. It's free and lets me upload photos and videos—and there is a group e-mail feature for storing friends and families' e-mail addresses. I love this one-click sharing feature." —*Aya*

**20** Zippers are always faster than snaps or (God forbid!) buttons. Buy a lot of cute one-piece rompers with one long zipper down the front and that can be worn day or night. You will save countless precious minutes (hours?) in the time it takes to dress your kid.

**21** Rather than repeatedly packing up your car with everything imaginable for another trip to Grandma's, consider buying a few used items that can just stay at her house—perhaps a high chair, portable crib, and umbrella stroller, as well as a few bowls, cups or bottles, bibs, and a handful of books and toys. If you're going to a place more than three or four times a year, you might find the relatively small monetary investment in duplicate gear is worth the time and stress of loading everything up—and you can always sell or donate items when outgrown.

· · ·  ▬▬  ▬▬  ▬▬  · · ·

**22** Boiling feeding bottles is so last-generation. Let go of the constant sterilizing. Clean bottles, nipples, and pacifiers using the hottest setting on your dishwasher or simply wash with soap and hot water. If you must sterilize, invest in zip-top sterilization bags that go right into your microwave.

· · ·  ▬▬  ▬▬  ▬▬  · · ·

**23** There's no real need to heat up (or make your own!) baby food. It's fine straight out of the jar, and you won't have to dirty another dish.

· · ·  ▬▬  ▬▬  ▬▬  · · ·

**24** Take turns. It's the smartest, simplest way to buy yourself some time, and it's good for both parents (and for baby). Take turns on feedings, bedtimes, outings to the park, whatever. When it's your partner's turn, resist the urge to hover. Release control and enjoy some alone time while you can.

**25** If you're lucky enough to have a baby who is amenable to waking up slowly and on her own, there's no need to rush into the nursery to pick her up the first time you hear a peep. Feel free to relish a few extra minutes in the morning—and you might set a pattern that lasts for months or even years to come.

**26** Simple errands are much more time-consuming with a baby or young child in tow. If a childless friend happens to mention she'll be at Trader Joe's or Target, ask her to pick up the two or three things you need—even if they're not baby-related.

**27**

"Once my baby was old enough to eat solids, I used to toss a frozen waffle into her crib. It would buy me an extra fifteen minutes or more in the morning while she gnawed on it . . . and the mess was totally worth it." —*Louise*

**28** Wash all your family laundry together rather than spending unnecessary time separating out your baby's clothes and doing a separate load.

**29** If your baby takes a pacifier, put three or four into the crib at every nap and at bedtime. You'll save yourself the time of racing back and forth to retrieve one.

# 30. Hair Washing in a Hurry

The easiest way to save hair-washing time is to only do it when your child *really* needs it. When that day comes, tricks can help it go more quickly. Try:

 Flexible plastic visors to keep soap and water out of faces.

 Handheld shower nozzles, play-size buckets, or watering cans for rinsing hair (older kids might prefer to do this themselves).

 If your child doesn't have much hair, don't even douse it. Try a sponge or washcloth to wet hair without her even fully realizing it, then a bit of shampoo, then rinse the same way.

 If your child's hair truly needs conditioner, try either a conditioning shampoo *or* put both the shampoo and the conditioner on her hair at the same time. Rinse only once.

 Ask your child to look up (quick!) at Tinkerbell, a fruit bat, butterfly, or other favorite flying creature—while you rinse in a flash.

Invest in a yummy-smelling, kid-friendly detangler spray. "Magic hair potion" can be an incentive to get that hair washed quickly (older kids can even spray it on themselves while still in the tub) and make the post-wash comb-through much less traumatic.

 Remember, everything's better with a goofy name or silly song to go with it. Instead of hair-washing time (said through clenched teeth), announce the opening of Dragon Scale Wash or Mermaid Palace Salon, then bring on the nonsense lyrics. (Pretty much anything can be sung to the old "Car Wash" tune.)

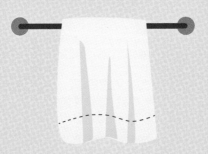

**31** Cook the family meal together, even if it means separating out portions with no spice. (If you're making chicken curry for the adults, set aside some cooked chicken, potatoes, and veggies for your child to eat, or freeze for later.) You'll save a lot of time by not custom making meals for every member of the family, and almost anything can be mashed or blended for new eaters.

* * * — — — * * *

**32** If your new baby is not prone to diaper rash, don't automatically change his diaper at the middle-of-night feedings. Unless you can smell #2, a wet diaper can usually wait until morning—and you can avoid waking baby more than necessary. (If your baby tends to have big nighttime pees, try a larger-size diaper, cinched snugly, to get through until morning without leakage—and without having to change a crib sheet.)

* * * — — — * * *

**33** If you've been reading stories at every nap and at bedtime, try out audio books. Classics such as *Frog and Toad* or *Little Bear* are readily available at your local library; pop one into the CD player and make your exit.

* * * — — — * * *

"We like to cook meals from scratch as much as possible, but when we can't (or when someone's belly won't wait), I keep certain things stocked to be able to throw something together quickly without it being a whole microwave meal deal. Buckwheat soba, rice sticks, penne, alphabet noodles; frozen turkey meatballs; and spinach. I also make extra of anything baby likes that is great for next day (for example, chicken breast . . . turns to chicken salad the next day). These things can all be tossed together really easily in a pinch!" —*Kim*

**35** During warm months, keep spare sunscreen and/or sun hats in your backyard, stroller, and car so it isn't an ordeal to stop what you're doing to hunt them down.

"We found a great inflatable toddler bed, which is much less bulky to travel with than a portable crib. We just keep it in the trunk of our car at all times, and we're ready for a full day at a friend's house or an overnight at Grandma's." —*Jackie*

**37** Who wants to go home at 7 p.m. just because it's baby's bedtime? When visiting friends, don't be afraid to put your baby down to sleep there, and then transfer her home several hours later. Young babies can snooze right in their car seat in another room, or bring along a portable crib for older babies and toddlers. They sleep deeply and might make the transfer to the car and then to your house without even waking.

# Little Lifesaver: Masking Tape

*A roll of masking or electrician's tape is a MacGyver Mom's best friend. Keep it stocked at home, in your bag, and in your car; use it for:*

- ✱ Covering electrical outlets at home, at a friend's house, or in a motel room

- ✱ Softening hard corners of tables and islands

- ✱ Covering the minute numbers on a digital clock, so your child can focus on the hour ("We're leaving when that reads 4," "You can get up when you see a 6")

- ✱ Making a commando bib out of a restaurant napkin

- ✱ Attaching butcher paper to any table or floor for art time

- ✱ Repairing endless torn books, broken wands, and the like

- ✱ Covering up the speaker on noisy toys

- ✱ Entertainment in planes, trains, and automobiles

**38** During potty training and shortly thereafter, keep a small stand-alone potty in the back of your car, neatly avoiding the time and stress of hunting down a bathroom on road trips, at the park, or on unexpectedly long outings around town.

* * * — — — * * *

**39** Some kids take forever to finish a meal. No one wants to encourage food gobbling, but sometimes you really need to wrap it up. Try a little side betting: "Do you think you need five minutes or six minutes to finish everything on your plate?" Act astonished at your child's answer, whatever it is. Then show her the numbers on the clock and see if she can "win."

* * * — — — * * *

**40**

"Get a dog—you'll save yourself hours of cleaning food off the floor." —*Jack*

---

**41** Car seat struggles may plague you as soon as your child begins to realize his independence, and cajoling or wrestling a toddler during every buckle-in can make you late (and frustrated) for any outing. To speed things up, offer simple incentives before you reach the car that are customized to your child: first pick of a song on the CD player, a special toy that comes out only in the car, or your agreement that he can pull his shoes off once he's seated. Older kids can be given the job of making sure *everyone* is buckled up, which can make them feel both important *and* cooperative.

**42**

"At ages one and two, the arched backs and fight against the car seat made it feel impossible to get going. This is where good behavior rewards began. With my son I used reward stickers: one sticker when you get in nicely and wait for me to buckle you. Now we use Tic Tacs, and both kids hop up quickly and sit nicely for a single treat." —*Simone*

**43** Many new moms complain about not being able to find the time to shower. Try bringing your baby to the bathroom with you, in his car seat or bouncer, and play peek-a-boo or sing a happy song. When your baby is sitting up, put a ring-style plastic tub seat (the kind with suction cups on the bottom) in your shower, along with a few tub toys that only live there. Toddlers and preschoolers often love playing in the shower with watering cans or sponges. Added bonus: You can check bath time off your list for later!

**44** Take yourself off of refill duty. If you hardly ever get the time to sit for a meal because you're constantly returning to the fridge, invest in a small pitcher with a lid and hand this task to pre-schoolers. They get practice pouring milk, water, or juice for themselves and other family members, and you might even get a hot meal.

• • • ━━ ━━ ━━ • • •

**45** Fill small, individual silicone cups (like the cupcake kind) or small measuring cups (like the ones that come with medicine) with the proper amount of maple syrup, soy sauce, ketchup, raisins, or other condiments that you would otherwise have to keep retrieving for your child. Let him know it's his job to dole them out, and when the cups are empty, it's done.

• • • ━━ ━━ ━━ • • •

**46** The first time you travel with your baby or child, create a master packing checklist and save it on your computer or in your journal. Include everything: clothes, toys, loveys, gear (carrier, monitor, booster seat, portable cribs and bedding, etc.), and number of diapers or bottles, if using. Congratulate yourself when you revisit this document for future trips.

**47** Children can make a simple walk to the mailbox take *foreeeever*. This is great when you are willing to turn this task into an adventure, but a problem if you have somewhere to be. When you can't get your child to get moving, turn it into a game. Challenge her to hop over or count cracks in the sidewalk, start stomping like a dinosaur or marching like you're in a parade, have her hold on to you and become a choo-choo train, or pretend you're following a line of caterpillars or ladybugs that only you can see.

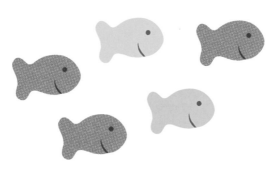

**48** Buy all your typical snacks—Goldfish crackers, pretzels, raisins, teething biscuits, etc.—in bulk and then divvy a lot of it into snack-size bags as soon as you get home. You'll save time *and* money, the snacks won't go stale like a big bag of them will, and you'll be ready to grab-and-go in a snap.

●　●　●　▬▬　▬▬　▬▬　●　●　●

**49** Use nap time to your advantage, as it may be the only free time of your day. Resist the urge to fill this time with chores that you could do while baby is awake. Instead, use at least three nap times each week to have guilt-free and luxurious personal time—shop online, take a solo bath, make phone calls to beloved friends, read, watch a movie, cook in peace.

●　●　●　▬▬　▬▬　▬▬　●　●　●

**50** Designate a pair of kitchen scissors as "food scissors," and quickly cut down your toddler's food without constantly getting out the knife and cutting board.

●　●　●　▬▬　▬▬　▬▬　●　●　●

**51** Wrestling crib sheets on and off is a pain. Instead, use a waterproof crib pad that attaches over your baby's regular sheet. In case of a midnight leak, you can just pull the pad off without having to replace the sheet. (And forget about using a crib bumper, no matter how cute they look!)

**52** You don't really need a changing pad plus a removable cover on your changing table (or whatever you're using as one). Buy a washable pad or just put a small towel on top, and stop wasting time getting the cover on and off.

**53** To find the time to blow-dry your hair or complete other bathroom activities, keep a low drawer or bin stocked with easy yet interesting child-safe items that you rotate frequently: a couple of bath toys, an animal-shaped washcloth, a small board book, a clean moisturizer jar or plastic bottle, a plastic sand timer from a board game, even an empty toilet paper roll.

**54**

"My kids love their gummy vitamins, which look and taste just like Gummi Bears. I tell them that the first one to get their shoes on or get in the car gets to pick out the color. Easy and effective—and something I was going to give them anyway." —*Kelli*

**55** Whenever you're trying to get kids to speed up, simply shake a container of snacks, which works exactly like a puppy hearing kibble hit the dish.

**56** Have your child help you give her toys a "bath." Put a dish tub or plastic bucket full of sudsy water on the floor of your shower or tub (or outside in nice weather), and get all those grimy plastic toys clean while also keeping your toddler entertained.

**57** Put a spiral notebook in a handy place to serve as a simple baby/child log for any caregivers to use. This way, everyone knows the baby's activities each day, including details about naps, bottles or meals, and outings. Also print out a current rundown of your baby's typical day from morning to night, and affix it to the inside front cover so you don't have to always write it down or explain it to others. It will get you out the door quicker any time a babysitter comes, and will save you time and worry over and over again.

• • • —— —— —— • • •

**58** If any sort of daily routine is getting too long and unwieldy—mealtime, bedtime, bath, drop-offs, getting out the door—bite the bullet and slash it. For example, if somehow you've increased from two bedtime books to four, go back to two—cold turkey. If it's taking too long to choose shoes, leave one pair by the door and hide the rest. After a few days of transition or protest (or maybe not), you'll save immeasurable time, energy, and stress.

• • • —— —— —— • • •

"Lots of dads want to find time to watch golf on weekends. Lots of kids need to nap. Instead of insisting on your child napping in his room, multitask *and* give Mom a break by snuggling up with your kid on the couch, where the quiet hum of golf patter is a great sedative." —*Scott*

**60** You will no longer have oodles of time to pamper yourself, so develop some quick ways to recharge when you find yourself with a free half hour: do yoga, take a bath by candlelight, write in a journal, read a great book, make a root beer float, paint your toenails, shoot baskets, make a fresh pot of coffee and cinnamon toast—whatever quick and easy thing makes *you* feel taken care of. You'll feel recharged and ready to enjoy your child when she wakes up or comes back from her outing with Grandma.

**61** Children of all ages love to race. And they hate to lose—especially to a parent! Use this to your advantage and challenge your child to a race to get up the stairs, into the store, from the car into the house, to put on pajamas, jackets, or shoes, or anything else you can think of.

**62** Teach "Simon Says" early and use it to speed up any tasks that you ask of your child (from climbing into a car seat to bringing a dish to the sink), or to keep a squirmy kid occupied on the changing table: "Simon says put your hands on your head. Simon says touch your nose. Simon says stick out your tongue." Voilà! Simon says the diaper is on.

**63** Keep your car stocked with a few essentials, and you'll save the time of constantly packing your diaper bag every time you leave the house—plus you'll save an unwanted trip home or to the store if you realize you're missing something essential, like wipes or a pacifier.

**64** Use your pediatrician's nurse line for all manner of health and development questions. You will often be able to save a trip to the doctor. (And it is *much* more efficient—and reliable—than hunting down information online.)

• • • — — — • • •

**65** Teach your toddler to choose and put on her own training pants—there's a reason they call them "Pull-Ups" and "Easy Ups," right?

• • • — — — • • •

# Little Lifesaver: Open Bins

*These will constitute the most prevalent storage system in your house for years to come. Embrace them—and teach your kids to use them, too! Use bins for storing:*

- Shoes and socks by the front door

- Seasonal items—hats, gloves, sunglasses, sunscreen—by the front door

- Backyard items—gardening tools, flip flops, outdoor toys—by the back door

- "Nature box" treasures—dandelions, rocks, leaves, and sticks your child would like to bring indoors—on a porch or balcony

- Toys or other items to go upstairs or downstairs

- Diapers, wipes, sanitizer, and other baby essentials

- Books and toys for the car

- General book, toy, and puzzle storage

- Gear for sports or classes

- Homework and lunch boxes

- Clothing and accessories

- Art supplies

**66**

"In warm weather, feed your baby in just her diaper and, when the messy meal is done, carry her *in* the high chair outside. Pour a pitcher of warm water over everything. She has fun in the water, the food bits get washed away, and everything gets carried inside nice and clean." —*Deb*

**67** Get the simplest molded-plastic high chair you can find (hello, IKEA!), with no cushions or extra belts for gooey food to hide. You will save yourself countless hours of unnecessary cleaning of all those nooks and crannies, and we've never heard a child complain about wanting a softer, squishier high chair.

**68**

"When I hang up my son's clothes, I hang up the shirt, then I slide the belt loop of a pair of pants or shorts over the hanger part. He's almost five years old now, and we've been doing this for several years. He's been able to go get dressed by himself forever, and I think this helps! It saves on drawer space, too!" —*Dot*

**69** If your child stalls putting on a certain clothing item (and whose doesn't?), let a favorite animal toy "pick out" the diaper or undies, pajamas, clothes, socks, or shoes—whatever you're having most trouble with. You'll see that polar bear or fuzzy bunny gets a lot less flak than you do.

**70** One-dish meals for your child save both prep and cleanup time. Put meat and veggies right in with the noodles or rice and serve.

* * * ▬ ▬ ▬ * * *

**71** Keep an updated phone list handy with not only emergency numbers, but numbers that you always seem to have to stop and hunt for: other parents in your child's school or day care, neighbors, preschool teachers, favorite babysitters, and stores or other locales you frequent.

* * * ▬ ▬ ▬ * * *

**72** Type the days and hours of your favorite recurring outings and events—like story time at the library, open gym, or toddler time at the zoo—into your electronic calendar, or keep a running list handy. That way, if you're wondering what to do on a rainy Wednesday morning, you can see options at a glance and be ready to roll.

* * * ▬ ▬ ▬ * * *

**73** Always carry wipes or sanitizer for times when you can't wait for a bathroom sink.

* * * ▬ ▬ ▬ * * *

# 74. "I Can Do It Myself!"

This phrase may be the most exciting thing you hear from your child, because it gives you a brief glimpse into a future when you don't do absolutely everything. As soon as your child is walking, start putting appropriate items at his level so you can begin the (long, arduous, but ultimately time-saving) process of teaching independence. It may seem like a lot of effort up front, but the payoff of future time and energy saved is immense—and, oh yes, it's important for your child's development, too. Try these to start:

 Set up a shoe cubby and reachable coat rack or peg near the door. A child as young as one year old can learn to put her shoes away and hang up her coat—and will enjoy doing it.

 Invest in good stools for all sinks so a toddler can learn to wash her own hands. (If she can't reach the faucet valves, try extending the cold tap by attaching a wooden spoon or measuring spoon to it with duct tape—not pretty, but a big time-saver for you.)

 Stock a low drawer with her cups, bowls, plates, and utensils, and ask her to pick things out and set her place before meals.

Have him help put all his toys (or socks, or books) into low shelves or open bins in his room at the end of each day.

 Work on self-dressing and brushing her own teeth and hair.

 As soon as your child is out of a high chair, make it a habit that he bring his plate or cup to the sink after a meal.

 When he's physically ready, allow him to climb in and out of his car seat.

**75** Swallow your pride and ask for a cut in line (at the grocery store, security line, or public bathroom) when you are dealing with a hungry baby, screaming toddler, or preschooler who *really* has to go.

• • • ▬▬ ▬▬ ▬▬ • • •

**76** A child who learns that it's fun to flip through a book *on his own* will free up your time immeasurably. Work on this early by putting appealing books at his level in different parts of the house, offering them as a reward ("You did such a good job putting your shoes away! Why don't you pick out your favorite book?"), and letting him see *you* reading ("I'm flipping through the pages of my book. Can you do it like mommy?"). Keep a bin or shoe box of books next to the potty and in the car that he can have access to when you're not available to read to him, and he'll quickly learn it's fun to "read" all by himself.

• • • ▬▬ ▬▬ ▬▬ • • •

**77** Interesting child-safe magnets at kid level can be a great time-saver in the kitchen. If your stainless-steel appliances aren't magnetic, put up a magnet board or a chalkboard. Ask your child to draw you somethhing or put all the animal magnets in a row, while you chop foods or put groceries away.

• • • ▬▬ ▬▬ ▬▬ • • •

**78** Some young children prefer frozen corn and peas right out of the bag, rather than thawed or cooked. Others like soft canned vegetables such as green beans or carrots right out of the can. Experiment and save yourself both prep time and pan cleanup.

• • • ▬▬ ▬▬ ▬▬ • • •

**79** Offering too many choices can be a big time waster, as kids can weigh and debate every option, then change their minds. Keep choices simple, direct, and finite: "Would you like to wear the red shirt or the blue shirt?" or "Would you like toast or cereal?" When you're really in a hurry, don't offer a choice—just give them what you want to give them, without opening things up for discussion.

• • • ▬▬ ▬▬ ▬▬ • • •

"Shoes go in a metal box near the front door so we can find them. Hats, gloves, and scarves have their own box. In the summer, I switch out the winter things and put sunglasses, sun hats, baseball caps, flip flops, etc., in the boxes. I can't tell you how much time this simple fix has saved me." —*Camille*

**81** To avoid drawn-out dressing issues, paste pictures of your child's clothes on the outside of the drawer or bin where they reside—i.e., a picture of a shirt on the shirt drawer, a picture of socks and underwear on that drawer, a picture of pajamas on that drawer. You might find you're now able to say, "Please go get a different shirt" or even "Please go get dressed," without having to drop everything to help—or having to wait twenty minutes for your child to remember where his shirts are (getting sidetracked along the way).

**82**

"I buy the same bobby socks for my three-year-old daughter and my one-year-old boy. I just fold them over when she is wearing them and leave them up when he is wearing them. It saves me tons of time when I have to match up socks or get them on in the mornings." —*Ruth*

 **83** Whenever you are pouring drinks, fill the lunch bottles or to-go cups for the next day.

 **84** Whenever you are cutting up fresh fruits or vegetables, cut some extra and pack them up for an upcoming meal or snack.

"With two kids in elementary school, I've made a wrapping station out of an old suit bag. I put rolls of wrap, plus ribbon, tissue, cards, scissors, and tape inside and zip it up; it stores easily in any closet, and I don't waste time hunting things down every time." —*Erin*

**86** Prep tomorrow's lunches while you're making dinner. For further ease, keep lunches on a basic schedule: Monday is pb&j, Tuesday is bagels and hummus, Wednesday is pasta, Thursday is soup, etc. The more variables you can remove, the faster things will go.

**87** Birthday parties are a (seemingly constant) part of your world as a parent. It's never too early to start a "gift closet," even if it has to live in your garage or under your bed. If you spot a good game, toy, or book on sale—buy several and stash them. If your child gets a duplicate present, put it there, too. Keep some wrap and recycled gift bags and tissue in the same place, and you have fast and easy one-stop shopping on birthday-party day.

• • • ━━ ━━ ━━ • • •

**88** If you find a pair of shoes your child likes, buy two pairs at once, in consecutive sizes, and save the time and headache of shoe shopping again in a few short months.

• • • ━━ ━━ ━━ • • •

**89**

"Since my daughter loves to help Mommy out, we bought a handheld vacuum small enough for her to use on her own. Keeps her busy and helps me out at the same time." —*Amanda*

**90** Most kids (and parents) love smoothies made with fruit, yogurt, and juice—and smoothies offer a great opportunity to hide some vegetables too, whether in the form of veggie juice or frozen spinach. But they can seem too time-consuming when rushing out the door on a weekday. Fill your blender with ingre-dients the night before and put it in the fridge so all you have to do is press "blend" when you wake up.

**91** Every weekend, plan at least four meals for the coming week and go shopping once.

# 92. Little Helpers

Believe it or not, toddlers and young children can actually help *save* you time now and then! Enlist your children to do the following household tasks, and you'll be building their esteem while saving yourself time:

 Carry light grocery bags in from the car

 Choose their dishes for mealtime and put them in the sink or dishwasher after the meal

 Help dry pots and pans or unload child-safe items from the dishwasher

 Set the table

Make their own bed (in their own special way)

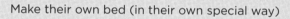 Make their own sandwich

Butter toast

Tear lettuce for salad

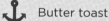 Mix or toss salads and pastas

 Refill their own drink from a child-safe small pitcher

Wash their own dishes in soapy water

 Help sort laundry (darks from lights before it goes in, whose clothes are whose when you're folding)

 Put their own laundry away into bins or drawers

 Assist in measuring, stirring, cracking eggs, and more during baking

 Help put away toys, clothes, and books at day's end

 Restock staples such as paper towels, wipes, and diapers around the house

Sweep with a child-size broom and dustpan

Water plants

Wash outdoor toys or bath toys

"Let kids help you with everyday tasks. There's no need for tons of fancy toys to fill your afternoons. As soon as Simon was able to stand on his own, we would prop him up on a chair against the kitchen counter and give him his own little bowl and spoon to pretend cook alongside us. We give him a wet cloth to wipe the table, a broom to sweep, and let him 'fold' the laundry. These make for fun, simple games to play with the kids." —Jackie

**93** Reserve library books online so you always have a stack of favorites waiting when you don't have time to browse.

• • • ━━ ━━ ━━ • • •

**94** Avoid shopping in unfamiliar stores where you don't know the layout like the back of your hand.

• • • ━━ ━━ ━━ • • •

**95** Rather than standing over your child during every hand washing, teach her to sing the ABC or happy birthday song on her own—when the song is done, her hands are done.

• • • ━━ ━━ ━━ • • •

**96** If you have CDs, audio books, or DVDs that your child is allowed to use on her own, set up a small station with the player, headphones, and a chair—and let her be in charge.

• • • ━━ ━━ ━━ • • •

**97** If running out to a toy store, bookstore, or superstore for a very specific item, always call ahead to see if it's in stock—and ask for it to be held for you at the front, and gift-wrapped if desired.

• • • ━━ ━━ ━━ • • •

**98** Play "shoe store" or "astronaut boots," or invent a special silly song for the often ridiculously challenging task of putting on and taking off socks and shoes. (While you're at it, get the simplest shoes with the easiest one-strap Velcro closure you can find.)

* * *  ▬▬  ▬▬  ▬▬  * * *

**99** To buy yourself some occasional, much-needed kid-free time, create games and activities that will entertain your child while you do something else (or simply remain on the couch). Create a simple obstacle course and time her as she goes through it over and over; rehide those plastic Easter eggs and see if she can find them all (make sure some are *really* hard!); ask her to figure out how many baby steps it takes to get from the front door to the back door; suggest she play "spies" and sneak around the house without you detecting her presence. You get the idea.

**100** As much as possible, shop and run errands on weekdays and at "off times"—after most children in town are dropped off at school and before they are picked up. Hitting grocery stores, discount chains, and drugstores during the late morning or early afternoon means less time standing in lines behind families with large carts.

**101** If you have a flight to catch or other reason to be moving early the next morning, dress your child in her next-day clothes (comfy ones, of course) *before* she goes to bed. You save dressing time *and* pajama-washing time. It might even become a habit in your house!

**102** Showers are quicker than tubs, especially if your child is one who adores the bath and has to be wrestled out of it.

. . . ━━ ━━ ━━ . . .

**103** Standing in long lines with young children can be a major headache. If you're planning an outing to a popular attraction—a zoo, aquarium, or theme park—call ahead and ask visitor services whether there are field trips or other unusually large groups scheduled for that day (these are often on spring Fridays). Arriving before 10 a.m. also usually gets you in ahead of the masses.

. . . ━━ ━━ ━━ . . .

**104** If your laundry room can support it, consider adding shelves or stacking bins, and keep the majority of your child's clothing there, to save yourself the time of transporting and putting everything away —especially if her room is on another floor.

. . . ━━ ━━ ━━ . . .

"I keep three small laundry bins in my son's room: one is for dirty clothes, one is for clothes he's outgrown that I want to keep, and one is for clothes he's outgrown that I want to donate or bring to the next kids' clothing swap. After I wash and fold laundry, I toss the outgrown clothes into their proper bins. Once a month I put the clothes I'm keeping into storage, and the ones I'm donating or swapping go to a thrift store or to the next clothing swap. It keeps his drawers from being too full of stuff he can't wear!" —*Erin*

**106** Weeding out outgrown or unloved clothes can eat up a huge amount of time, starting in infancy. Hang a basic laundry bag behind your child's door in which you toss clothes that she no longer wears, and save yourself the time of digging through those items over and over again when you're in a hurry to get out the door. When the bag gets full, it's time to donate or consign (or store if you're expecting another child).

• • • ━━ ━━ ━━ • • •

**(107)** Keep a limited number of weather-appropriate pajama choices in the bathroom where your child gets ready for bed. This will save you the back-and-forth to his room, during which many children get distracted, stall, or end up in a Halloween costume instead of their jammies.

• • • ━━ ━━ ━━ • • •

# Little Lifesaver: Timer

A timer with a buzzer or bell is an essential part of your parenting toolbox, because you will constantly be telling your children how much time they have to do things before you blow your top—or to win a reward. (A sand timer from any board game can also be used in a pinch for stationary jobs such as toothbrushing or hand washing.) You can use the timer in a straightforward way to signal the end of something, but you can also use it to turn tasks into a fun "beat the clock" game. Either way, the added bonus is that it takes the unpleasant responsibility away from Mom or Dad—what the timer says, goes! Here are some times when it's useful to have a timer:

- To signal when it's time to leave the house for school or an activity

- To signal the end of a playdate or trip to the park

- To signal the end of video or computer time

- To announce a meal

- To aid in toy sharing (each child can have it for XX minutes)

- 🌟 For getting dressed in the morning

- 🌟 For getting shoes, socks, and jackets on

- 🌟 For sluggish mealtimes (how long they have to finish if they want dessert, for example, or how fast they need to wrap up breakfast if they want to pick the first song in the car)

- 🌟 For completing a task such as putting toys away and turning the chore into a game

- 🌟 For getting ready for bed

- 🌟 For brushing teeth

- 🌟 For washing hands

• • • ▬ ▬ ▬ • • •

"When we're getting ready to go somewhere, I set the timer for five minutes and let the kids know, 'Listen for the bell!' When the timer rings, I yell, 'Hi, ho!' And we start singing, 'Hi, ho, hi, ho it's off to _____ we go' and march out the door." —YUMI

**108** Always pick out clothes the night before, whether you give your child a choice in the outfit or not. Lay out absolutely everything she will need, all the way down to the socks, headband, or belt.

• • • ▬▬ ▬▬ ▬▬ • • •

**109** If you can stand it, avoid cleaning up the same family clutter ten times a day. Pick one or two times of day to do a sweep—say, lunchtime and bedtime—and drop everything into baskets or bins.

• • • ▬▬ ▬▬ ▬▬ • • •

**110** If your child is involved in classes or team sports, designate a box or bin in a central place as the receptacle for all of the related gear—ballet shoes, shin guards, baseball glove, etc. Create another bin for homework when the time comes. This cuts down on the constant "Mom, where is my _____ ?" and the time spent hunting for it when you're already late.

• • • ▬▬ ▬▬ ▬▬ • • •

**111** Keep kid-safe arts and crafts supplies within your child's reach. There's no reason you should have to drop everything to fetch paper and crayons again and again.

• • • ━━ ━━ ━━ • • •

**112** Don't overbook your time—or your child's. Rather than expending an inordinate amount of time and energy getting to a half-hour class or outing that your child's not really interested in yet, allow yourself a chance to just hang out with her and not have to hustle.

• • • ━━ ━━ ━━ • • •

## 113

"We take turns at parties and other social events that we go to as a family. We agree on one hour each to socialize with our friends while the other plays with the kid. This was after many parties where I felt so frustrated and tired of being on-call as a mom and not being able to catch up with friends." —*Mariale*

**114** Always look for a family lane at airports and other stations—if you don't see one, ask.

**115** When your cashier asks if you need help out today, say yes. You still have to lug all that stuff into your house and unpack it all with a kid in tow, so you might as well save yourself some time loading it into your own car!

**116** Put small sealed bowls or zip-top bags of appropriate snacks in a low cupboard for your child to reach on his own, as well as a small pitcher or sippy cup of milk, water, or other beverage on the low shelf of your fridge. Young kids can fetch their own cereal, granola bar, or juice, and enjoy doing it.

- - - ▬▬ ▬▬ ▬▬ - - -

**117** When your child first starts sleeping all night in underpants, make the bed like this: waterproof mattress pad / fitted sheet / second waterproof mattress pad / second fitted sheet. If she wakes up wet and crying at 2 a.m., pull one set off and the second set is waiting. (Very heavy sleepers might allow you to do this without fully waking!) It's much, much faster than removing her from bed and replacing all the bedding.

- - - ▬▬ ▬▬ ▬▬ - - -

**118** Arrange a "me-time" schedule with your spouse or partner, when each of you gets a couple hours of guilt-free time to do whatever you like each weekend—at a time of day that works best for the whole family. It's a good way to refresh and maintain balance as not only a parent, but a person.

● ● ● ━━ ━━ ━━ ● ● ●

**119** Transitions of any kind are tough on toddlers and young children, and they can revolt if they feel blindsided—making the move take even longer. Always give several notices for any change in activity in order to leave on schedule—i.e., don't think you can tell your kids it's time to finish up at the playground and actually be in your car moments later. Instead, give them a five-minute, three-minute, and one-minute warning to wrap up. For kids too young to understand time, offer a set number of activities before it's time to leave (three more trips down the slide, five more jumps through the sprinkler, one more song on the radio).

● ● ● ━━ ━━ ━━ ● ● ●

**120**

"I spent an inordinate amount of time and effort in arguing with my daughter that tutus or dress-up shoes were not 'outdoor clothes.' Then I realized that at age four, pretty much anything is acceptable. So unless it's shorts in the snow, she can wear what she likes and we get out the door a lot faster." —*Stacy*

**121** During months when your kids are in and out of the yard, keep a shoe bin and a foot-washing station by each door, as well as a large open basket for dumping all the outdoor toys at day's end. Kids can be responsible for picking up and washing up before dinner, and you'll save a ton of cleanup time every evening.

Any way you slice it, kids cost a lot of dough. In fact, if someone calculated for you ahead of time exactly what the total expense would be, you might have had a panic attack—and then a long, long talk with your partner about whether the whole enterprise was such a good idea. But while it might not be entirely rational, or financially prudent, we go forth as parents: It's all about love, after all, and you can't put a price tag on that.

Still. Wouldn't it be nice if expensive art supplies didn't dry out, dolls weren't left on airplanes, shoes were never outgrown, and Goldfish crackers were free? Sure. Until that day, though, save a few bucks in your piggy bank by trying out some tips from parents who have figured out how to get through the week with enough cash left over for pizza and movies with the family on Friday night. Really, at the end of the day, who could ask for anything more than that?

**122** When planning for baby, buy or register for only the basics you'll need for the first few weeks (onesies, diapers, bottles, blankies, car seat) and ask for gift cards for the rest. In a few months, you'll have a much better sense of what you need—and the money will be put to much better use than if you rush out and buy everything before the baby comes.

· · · —— —— —— · · ·

**123** Thrift stores are filled with brand-new baby items that a mom never got around to returning. Don't let this happen to you! Label a large manila envelope or accordion file for baby/child receipts as soon as possible (ideally, starting with the gift receipts from your baby shower). Throw every receipt related to your child into the envelope or file, or set up an electronic filing system, so when a gift is the wrong size or you realize you hate the shoes you bought online, you can get a refund or at least a credit.

· · · —— —— —— · · ·

**124**

"I finally realized Goodwill isn't just for gear and furniture, it has great kids' clothes, too, for very little money . . . especially in the richer neighborhoods where barely used quality stuff gets donated regularly." —*Annie*

**125** Remember the holy trifecta: Goodwill. Craigslist. Consignment store. Never buy anything new for your child until you've scoured these three sources and then asked at least three friends (who will likely offer the item for free in return for getting it out of their own house).

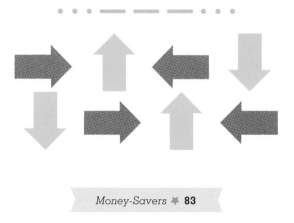

# 126. Hospital Takeaways

You're paying a lot of money for that hospital stay when you deliver your baby. It only makes prudent financial sense to take home everything you can, so make sure there's some room in your overnight bag. Here are some examples of handy items to hang on to:

 Those weird disposable panties (why soil your own?)

 Mega maxi-pads

 Large plastic cup with lid and bendable straws, to keep mom hydrated

 No-slip slipper socks (great for climbing stairs in the middle of the night)

 Pacifiers

 Formula samples (even if you're not planning to use them; you never know)

 Baby lotion, wash, or wipe samples

"I have to admit that we took home the plastic 'vomit tub' that was by the bed at the hospital. Our daughter was so small that it made a perfect infant bathtub for the first few weeks!" —Paul

 Nipple-soothing gel and/or lanolin

 Disposable breast pads

 Diapers

⚓ Swaddle blankets

⚓ Baby hats and/or onesies

⚓ Personal-care items such as toothpaste, mouthwash, and disposable toothbrushes that are in the hospital bathroom (great extras for when guests come to visit baby)

**127** Sling, ERGObaby, BabyBjörn, Moby—how are you supposed to know which pricey baby carrier is for you? Test out several types before committing by taking those belonging to friends for a spin, or by calling around to find out which stores allow you to try before you buy. Some mom-focused stores even offer one-on-one tutorials, baby-wearing classes, and/or a realistically weighted baby doll for practice. Even if you make as informed a decision as possible, keep the receipt for a possible exchange. Baby carriers are expensive but necessary, and you should have one you love.

**128** Use washable nursing pads. They don't take up much room in the laundry you're already doing, and they last indefinitely.

**129** Instead of an expensive nursing top with hidden openings, cut holes in an old T-shirt and layer it underneath whatever you're wearing. When you hike up your outer shirt to nurse, you won't be exposing more skin than you'd like.

**130**

"Cloth diapers make great inexpensive burp cloths—they are soft, absorbent, and durable. When they get worn, you can create 'lovey' blankets out of them with some stuffing, a needle, and colorful thread." —*Erin*

**131** Plastic measuring spoons and cups, attached by a ring, are the best stroller or car seat toy for babies—and can be found at any dollar or discount store.

**132** Babysitting swaps are a great way to save dough. If you're in a parents' group or have friends or neighbors with kids, swap some babysitting time to find a free afternoon or low-cost date night. You can even do this after the kids are in bed!

**133** You don't really need to buy pajamas for babies, or even toddlers. The soft pull-on pants and shirts they wear are essentially the same attire—if you have enough of these, just forget the extra purchase.

• • • ━━━ ━━━ ━━━ • • •

**134** Don't get sucked into pricey baby toys. Favorite "toys" can be scavenged from what you prob-ably already have around the house: sheer scarves, pots and pans with lids, wooden spoons, Tupperware of all sizes, metal mixing bowls, salad spinners, empty boxes, laundry baskets, water bottles (with caps removed or sealed tight), empty oatmeal containers, magazines and catalogs, kitchen timers, your old cell phone, TV remote control, sunglasses, keys, or digital camera. Make use of these things and save your money for when she's in kindergarten and has to have a Barbie scooter in order to survive.

• • • ━━━ ━━━ ━━━ • • •

**135** Turn your radio to static or turn on a fan and you have a no-purchase white-noise machine.

• • • ━━━ ━━━ ━━━ • • •

**136**

"While I'm working on my laptop, my daughter 'types' on an old computer keyboard I was going to throw away." —*Ann*

**137** A glue stick and some black and white construction paper will get you stimulating art for your newborn at a fraction of the cost of fancy black-and-white mobiles and artwork you see marketed for babies, who really don't care about whether it's perfectly executed.

**138** There's no need to invest in a $200 diaper bag. Chances are, you already have a messenger bag, backpack, or tote that you like—and that will work just fine. In fact, many people prefer nondiaper bags because they don't have so many little compartments where things can get misplaced.

**139** Sign up for free samples at a variety of baby Web sites. Your mailbox will start filling up with diapers, wipes, baby lotions, stain removers, and more—in convenient travel sizes you can take on the go—plus coupons, too!

* * * ▬▬ ▬▬ ▬▬ * * *

**140** As your baby grows, tape pictures torn from baby catalogs (or enlarged printouts of your digital family pics) on his wall or next to the changing table. You can even laminate favorites at any copy shop for more durability. They'll get more interest than that expensive print you've been considering because it matches the nursery decor.

* * * ▬▬ ▬▬ ▬▬ * * *

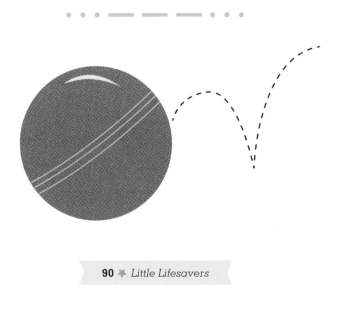

**141** Instead of a spendy glider or rocking chair, buy a $20 exercise ball. You'll strengthen your core, soothe your baby, and save money, all at the same time.

• • • ▬▬ ▬▬ ▬▬ • • •

**142** Borrow the most expensive (and temporary) baby gear—like a breast pump, crib, infant car seat, stroller, or glider—from a parent who might be "in between" kids, and return items when your baby outgrows them.

• • • ▬▬ ▬▬ ▬▬ • • •

**143** A clothing/gear swap is a great excuse for a get-together with your parents' group, neighbors, or family friends. Keep it simple: Ask everyone to bring one bag of clothes and one bag of books, toys, or other gear (including half-full packs of diapers!) that they are ready to pass on. Everything should be in good condition and ideally sorted by size. You might want each family to bring a snack to share, too. The host takes the responsibility of taking any unclaimed items to the charity of choice. In six months, do it again at another house.

• • • ▬▬ ▬▬ ▬▬ • • •

"We took our now almost four-year-old daughter to the zoo and the museum, etc., when she was younger, but she was only interested in the playground. It was frustrating to spend all day and about $80 to visit the zoo and she didn't even seem interested. I don't think any of it was worth it until now. Outings like running errands are all that she really needed to meet the outside world. She would ultimately prefer the undivided attention of her parents to shuttling around in the car all afternoon." —*Karissa*

**145** Don't buy a crib until you need one. Many babies sleep in a co-sleeping bassinet or smaller portable crib for several months at least. By then, you might come across one you can borrow or buy used—or ask for it as a first-birthday gift!

**146** Your baby or young child does not really need classes or lessons—unless *you* need them to add structure to your week. If you're at home, invite other at-home parents to come over for play dough or finger painting (free art class!), world music on the home stereo (free music class!), or dancing with scarves or bubbles in the backyard (free movement class!). Besides being gratis, these can be more fun and flexible for your child . . . plus you won't lose money for classes missed for colds or doctors' appointments. Added bonus: no dressing, packing, or schlepping baby to and from.

•  •  •  ▬▬  ▬▬  ▬▬  •  •  •

**147** Babies and young children not only accept repetition, they thrive on it. If you find that a certain outing is a favorite of both of yours—say the zoo or a toddler gym—buy a pass and make the most of it by going often.

•  •  •  ▬▬  ▬▬  ▬▬  •  •  •

**148** Figure out who in your neighborhood regularly offers free, healthy samples: grocer, bakery, cheese shop, farmers' market, etc. Samples are a great free snack for kids, *and* they get a kick out of them.

•  •  •  ▬▬  ▬▬  ▬▬  •  •  •

# Little Lifesaver: Zip-Top Bags

*Besides their usual kitchen usage, zip-top bags can save you over and over again as a parent when you're out and about. Say what you will about the environment— you need these, and to help save the Earth you can wash and reuse them (if the contents aren't too awful). They take so little room that you can keep a few extra empty ones in your car or bag, and you will find a use for them, whether it's to divvy up a large bag of Pirate's Booty or to cart home a wet pair of underpants. Use them to carry:*

- Wipes (much cheaper than buying travel-size packs)

- Wet paper towels for the car

- Snacks (there's really no need for snack bowls, and bags fold down when empty)

- Nipples and pacifiers (to avoid getting covered with crud in your bag)

- Bribes (such as emergency jelly beans, pennies, Tic Tacs, or stickers)

- Premeasured dry formula

- Dirty diapers

- Wet swimsuits

- Dirty or wet clothing

- Odds and ends of small beach or pool toys

- "Treasures" kids want to take home from out-of-doors

- Beach shoes

- Essentials for your stroller basket

- Any leaky or messy kid stuff, such as bubbles, paints, or markers

"Plastic bags of the zip-lock variety are the key to being ready for anything! I keep three to four of them, each filled with particular essential items, handy at all times. The beauty of these is that they take up very little room, and can be transferred easily from one diaper bag (or whatever it is that you are using for a diaper bag) to another. They can also be easily transferred from one parent to another, or to whoever may be looking after the little one. Just hand off and go." —RANDY

**149** Cable TV can be really pricey—and you probably don't watch a whole lot of it these days. Consider canceling cable and relying on DVDs from the library or Netflix—not only much cheaper, but also commercial-free to save you future purchasing battles with your kids.

**150** Any time you're at a restaurant that offers crayons to the kids, take 'em home—it's great to have extra sets in your bag and car for unexpected waits. While you're at it, you might as well take a few extras of the scribble-able place mats, too.

**151** Kids love water tables, but they're expensive and unwieldy to own. Make a makeshift version for your yard or front stoop by filling a shallow plastic dish tub with water and tossing in some funnels, plastic measuring cups, and waterproof toys. Bonus points for adding food coloring or bubbles! You can also try filling the tub with cornmeal, birdseed, or sand for a kid who loves to scoop.

**152** You will be doing a lot more housework and laundry than ever before. If you haven't already employed thrifty practices, now is the time. Make sure you're only using the suggested amount of detergent, and tear dryer sheets in half. Use washable cloths instead of paper towels. Run sponges through the dishwasher rather than tossing. Buy refillable bottles of hand soap, dishwashing liquid, and household cleaners. You get the idea.

· · · ▬ ▬ ▬ · · ·

**153** If you have an abundance of toys, consider asking family members for a savings bond or 529 plan contribution in lieu of a gift.

· · · ▬ ▬ ▬ · · ·

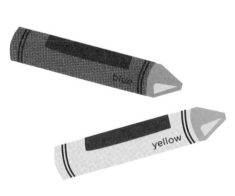

**154**

"For stocking stuffers and other incentive gifts, I often give items I would have spent money on anyway: McDonald's dollar books (they still make them, you just have to ask!), movie tickets, cool new toothbrushes, hair clips, tights and undies, Chuck E. Cheese tokens, etc. The kids get a present, and my budget stays the same." —*Erin*

**155** Many cities have community centers that offer low-cost playrooms and open gyms suitable for kids crawling through age five—havens on rainy days. For a couple bucks, you'll find trikes, scooters, balls, play kitchens, train tables, slides, and even bouncy houses.

**156** Forgo buying a separate "baby detergent." It's expensive and unnecessary, especially with good dye- and perfume-free detergent choices on the market.

· · · —— —— —— · · ·

**157** Many parents who ask to borrow big-ticket baby items still shy away from inheriting apparel such as clothes and shoes. But the truth is, many children have clothes in great condition that were hardly (or never!) worn, and parents love knowing that someone is using them. Put the word out to family and friends that your child is growing and you're now in the market for XX-size items, and see what goodies you might receive. If you don't know anyone with a child who can offer hand-me-downs, approach parents with a child the right age at your playgroup, day care, or on Craigslist to see if they're interested in passing on their outgrown items to you for a nominal fee. It may become a relationship that lasts for years.

· · · —— —— —— · · ·

**158** You will go through countless packages of wipes in your parenting career. As a substitute, try soaking clothlike paper towels in water and keeping them in a zip-top bag. Add a couple of drops of natural baby wash if you like. Added bonus: no chemicals to annoy sensitive skin.

· · · — — — · · ·

**159** There is no need to buy several bath products for your baby or young child. One simple, natural body wash functions well as a body cleanser, shampoo, and gentle bubble bath.

· · · — — — · · ·

**160** Buy plain generic diapers and training pants from the get-go. Once kids get hooked on having Elmo, Dora, or the Disney Princesses on their bottoms, there's no turning back. (Plus, this way you'll leave yourself an excellent bribe for potty training—characters on their underpants!)

· · · — — — · · ·

**161** Bare-bottom time (if you can deal with it, or if you can play outside much of the day) is an effective potty-training method that also saves you money.

· · · — — — · · ·

**162**

"Share, barter, and commit yourself to learning how to do more in your home instead of hiring it out. Friends are often fonts of wisdom and free stuff." —*Becky*

**163** Travel by plane before your baby turns two—especially to expensive destinations. The hassle of sharing your seat with baby still beats having to buy a full-price ticket.

**164** Even young babies love bubbles—and the rapture continues into grade school. Store-bought bubble solution might not seem expensive, but once your child dumps her fifteenth bottle on your lawn, your opinion might change. Try this: Mix 1 cup water with 2 tablespoons light corn syrup and 4 tablespoons liquid dish soap. Cut out the centers of plastic lids (from sour cream, salsa, or yogurt containers) to use as wands.

**165** The best bath toys around are already in your drawer or recycle bin. Try plastic containers of all sizes (poke holes in the bottom of some for a shower effect), empty shampoo bottles, plastic funnels, colanders, and measuring cups.

**166** Never toss those refillable plastic tubs that baby wipes come in. They make handy and secure storage for crayons, pencils, and other art supplies when you're on the go—as well as a free bin for play jewelry, coins, small toys, or just about anything.

**167** Wait as long as you can to decide on what stroller to buy: umbrella-style, jogger, travel system, etc. The secondhand stores are littered with strollers that turned out to be not quite the right thing for the parents who bought them while pregnant. Instead, use a simple Snap-N-Go to convert the infant car seat into a stroller and make your decision later, when you have a better sense of your needs.

**168** Trade one small bag of toys, books, dress-up stuff, or kids' DVDs with a neighbor or friend in your parents' group—even if it's just for a week or two. It's a great way to keep things fresh and interesting for free.

•  •  •  ▬▬  ▬▬  ▬▬  •  •  •

**169** Resist the urge to buy a bigger car the moment you find out you're pregnant. An average sedan provides plenty of room for two young kids and their stuff. The money you save in car payments, gas, and maintenance can be used to rent a minivan for a longer road trip when (and if) you need it.

•  •  •  ▬▬  ▬▬  ▬▬  •  •  •

**170**

"Bag Balm [originally developed for cow udders] works wonders on diaper rash; it's also helpful to use a hair dryer on the low setting to dry kiddo off completely, which might mean you don't need diaper cream at all." —*Lissa*

**171** If your child has dry, itchy skin or an irritated diaper area, frequently nothing is better than plain old baking soda in the bath. Try this a few times before moving on to more expensive alternatives.

**172** The little toys and candies (that your child doesn't plow through) in birthday-party goody bags, stockings, or Easter baskets are perfect for squirreling away in your car or bag for an instant surprise (a.k.a. bribe) in a sticky situation when you need cooperation—like in a long line, in a traffic jam, or at the end of a playdate when you're running late.

**173** Start a new tradition with your friends who have kids: Each person brings a recycled game or book from their house as a birthday-party gift rather than purchasing something new. Everyone's got something to pass on, and a two-year-old really doesn't need ten brand-new presents.

**174** Check your local used bookstore, consignment store, or Goodwill for children's books, and contact your library to find out when they're having book sales. Kids' books get trashed and chewed on anyway, so there's no need to buy them pristine.

**175** Consider LED lights for the nursery, especially if you leave the lights on at night.

**176** There will be a shocking amount of food that you prepare for your child that he chooses not to eat—day in, day out. Invest in a good set of very small food-storage containers with snap lids so you can bring it back out tomorrow.

**177** There is nothing wrong with day-old cookies and other baked goods. Your kid will go crazy for them just the same, at a fraction of the price.

**178** Get all your kids' DVDs at the library. It never fails that once you buy their favorite one, they lose interest in it almost immediately. Ditto on CDs.

**179** Don't throw away all those broken crayons—you'll have hundreds. Instead, toss small peeled pieces into mini-muffin tins (about a quarter full); bake at 300 degrees for about ten minutes or until all the wax is melted. When *completely* cooled, pop out good-as-new multicolored crayons in a fun new shape. (A full set of these in a pretty bag can also be a low-cost gift.)

**180**

"Picnic ware makes great inexpensive, durable storage for kids' stuff, and is often in brightly colored or patterned plastic. I have a flower-shaped chip-n-dip (to keep jewelry separate), a flatware caddy (for wands and lightsabers), condiment trays (for special rocks and various collectibles). Stock up at the end of summer when it all goes on sale." —*Erin*

**181** Repurpose the pretty wrap from each birthday gift received to make a homemade thank-you note from your child, using markers, ink stamps, and stickers you have around the house. This saves money and is a great craft activity, plus it involves your child in the art of good manners from a very early age.

**182** Keep a couple of "special" granola bars or breakfast cookies in your cupboard, car, or purse that your child doesn't normally have. That way, when you stop at your local coffee shop, you can reveal an exciting treat and avoid plunking down cash for a too-big pastry or muffin.

• • • ━━ ━━ ━━ • • •

**183** Most toddlers don't need a salon haircut. Trim bangs yourself and spring for a real cut only when desperate.

• • • ━━ ━━ ━━ • • •

**184** If your child is into art, save every scrap of gift wrap, tissue, and ribbon, as well as all fancy bags, cards, envelopes, and mailers that come into your house. It can all be repurposed and will save you big bucks at the craft store.

• • • ━━ ━━ ━━ • • •

**185** Ask your butcher for butcher paper, or hit a restaurant-supply store, rather than buying the craft version. IKEA and other wrap-it-yourself retailers are also great places to grab a few extra sheets of "art paper."

• • • ━━ ━━ ━━ • • •

**186**

"If your kid is a sticker fanatic, be sure to hide your pretty self-adhesive stamps— or you might end up with a $47 piece of art at the end of craft time." —Jenna

**187** It's okay to have a small apartment or house for your family. Babies and young children like to be in cozy spaces (an alcove or open closet works just fine as a nursery) and they really don't see any difference between your house and the Joneses'. Save the money for a time when you have a sense of how big your family is going to get and exactly what you want out of your living space.

**188** Stock up on seasonal stickers, toys, decorations, and other paraphernalia the day after a holiday. Little kids simply don't care if they're using bat stickers in November or a set of reindeer rubber stamps in January.

## 189

"My daughter already had a decent dress-up trunk at age three, so that was combed for Halloween rather than buying a new costume. Take advantage of that while they're little—once they hit elementary school, they'll probably be adamant about what character they want to be." —*Jessica*

**190** Start a Halloween costume exchange with your friends—even far-away families can swap by mail. There is no need to spend a lot on an outfit that will be worn for an hour and quickly outgrown—and many kids change their mind about wearing it when they're halfway out the door.

**191** Make your own play dough! It's cheaper, more pliable, and lasts longer, plus older kids can help with the "cooking" of it.

| | |
|---|---|
| 1 cup flour | 1 cup water |
| 1/2 cup salt | 2 teaspoons cream of tartar |
| 1 tablespoon oil | Food coloring |

Combine the dry ingredients in a small saucepan. Mix in the wet ingredients. Heat over low to medium heat, stirring constantly to prevent scorching, until the mixture forms into a ball (no more than 5 minutes). Remove from heat, knead until smooth, and store in a sealed plastic container.

* * * ━ ━ ━ * * *

**192** Every parent knows that diapers are expensive. Unless your child is rash-prone, don't be overly solicitous about changing a diaper or training pants every time it is slightly damp. The almost-too-effective, moisture-wicking technology in today's diapers keep baby dry. (Move to washable training pants—like underwear with an absorbent liner—as soon as your child is ready.)

* * * ━ ━ ━ * * *

**193** Young children rarely need special-occasion clothes—meaning they will surely have outgrown whatever you bought by the time the next event rolls around. Borrow a fancy outfit, coat, even shoes for that wedding—the mom who bought these at full price will likely be happy to know they were worn at least twice. Same goes for vacation items such as snowsuits or snorkeling gear.

* * * — — — * * *

**194** Have realistic expectations of what the "perfect" kid's room looks like. When you're decorating your child's room for the first time, you can go nuts looking at catalogs and buying significant pieces of art and furniture that really mean nothing to small children. They crave comfort, familiarity, and ease in their surroundings—not chandeliers and thousand-dollar bed frames.

* * * — — — * * *

"After moving our daughter to her pretty big-girl bed, she asked over and over again for her mattress to be on the floor—whether it was for monsters under the bed or what, we don't know. We finally did it, and she still loves it, almost two years later. Plus, now she and her younger sister can jump and tumble on the bed without us worrying about the height. Her room may look like a dorm, but I wish I'd put off buying that spendy bed frame in the first place!" —*Sandra*

**196** When your child is ready to move from the crib to a bed, start by just putting the crib mattress on the floor. It's a simple way to test out the transition before investing in a bed, and you don't have to invest in a frame and safety rails. Plus if you decide to go back to the crib for a few more months, it's a simple switch back.

"At any circus, carnival, or festival, there are really expensive light-up toys and snacks every few feet and stuffed animals everywhere. Knowing your kid's soft spot, avoid the meltdown by preloading a treat and picking up an inexpensive light wand or other toy before you go. You can even wrap it! Or, help your child carefully select a favorite stuffed animal from home to accompany your family and to see his or her friends at the carnival; you can even make them tickets." —*Simone*

**198** Throw all your veggie scraps—you'll have a ton of them over the coming months and years—into a freezer bag to later turn into an easy broth.

**199** When eating out, share an entrée with your child rather than paying for him to eat two bites of hot dog and three fries. Or pack along something you know he will like.

• • • ━━ ━━ ━━ • • •

**200** Many cities offer free or pay-what-you-can museum days one day per month. This is a great opportunity to introduce your young child to not only art but also the concept of a museum—without worrying if he will only last for thirty minutes.

• • • ━━ ━━ ━━ • • •

**201** It can be expensive to decorate for the holidays, especially with kids wanting to buy everything in sight. Instead, budget for a day-after spree and have your kids help you pick up great deals and package it for storage. Next year, it will seem brand-new at a fraction of the price.

• • • ▬▬ ▬▬ ▬▬ • • •

**202** Find a good kids' consignment store and establish a relationship with the staff. Not only will you find great deals, you'll earn store credit for everything you consign—which means low-cost birthday presents, baby-shower gifts, and goodies for your own kids. Plus, the staff who know you are often more amenable to answering phone queries about what's in stock and setting aside something they know you are looking for.

• • • ▬▬ ▬▬ ▬▬ • • •

**203** If you live near a college, check out lower-priced plays, concerts, and art shows that are appropriate for the family.

• • • ▬▬ ▬▬ ▬▬ • • •

**204**

"Check out indie record stores for free in-store concerts of bands that are probably playing at an expensive venue that night. The in-store shows are often kid-appropriate and really fun." —*Becky*

**205** Community or neighborhood centers are a terrific source of low-cost classes, workshops, and holiday events—from Easter egg hunts to Halloween festivals—that are appropriate for all ages. Get on the mailing list so you don't miss the fun.

**206** If you're not ready to invest in swimming lessons, take advantage of family swim times at your local pool instead. It's a good rainy-day activity for a fraction of the cost of a lesson.

**207**

"We finally realized that home stores like Home Depot and Loews often have craft time for kids on Saturday mornings—for free. The kids have fun and get to bring home a project—and we get our shopping done." —*Erin*

---

**208** Many tumbling gyms, gymnastics centers, and dance studios host "indoor playground" time for unstructured play, offering use of their space and equipment for a nominal fee. Also ask about a free trial class. (If you do enough free trial classes at different places around town, you might not need to pay for a class for several more months!)

**209** Story times at local libraries, bookstores, or cafés are almost always free and often include a craft or music element as well. They are held on different days and times in different neighborhoods—check them all out and find your favorite.

. . . —— —— —— . . .

**210** If you have an avid reader, teach your child about the beauty—and savings—of a good used bookstore by letting her trade in outgrown books for a fresh supply.

. . . —— —— —— . . .

**211** Keep track of "kids eat free" offers at your local restaurants, and patronize them for dinners out. Otherwise, go out for lunch or breakfast, which is always cheaper than dinner, or hit happy hour at family-friendly spots.

. . . —— —— —— . . .

**212** Walk where you can.

. . . —— —— —— . . .

**213**

"We hike and ramble and let our son bring home bugs, rocks, and sticks—these become treasures and toys that are used more than the stuff we buy. We store them in vintage jars from Value Village and Goodwill, and this actually doubled as a sorting/counting game when he was younger. He has one jar for shells, one for rocks, and one for various tree pieces/parts. Really rad stuff—like a snake molt and a wasp nest (and the latest cool find)—go in a little tray on his toy shelf with a magnifying glass." —*Becky*

**214** Split a CSA (Community Supported Agriculture) box with neighbors or friends, and you'll eat organic for less—and save yourself another trip to the store, where you'll probably buy more than you planned.

**215** Back up all your DVDs and use the copies as your active set. Little fingers and feet can quickly damage these appealing little shiny objects.

**216** Keep ice cream, cones, and sprinkles stocked at home to give kids special "ice cream parlor" treats while keeping costs down.

**217** Garden—whether in your yard, balcony, or local community garden. Not only is it great exercise and education for you and your child, you will save money on kid-friendly peas, cherry tomatoes, basil, or berries.

**218**

"After holidays (or as needed), pack away some underused toys and books. When they magically reappear, it's like having new toys without spending a dime. Just moving toys to different places (from upstairs to downstairs, for example) can often produce this effect." —*Catherine*

**219** If you invest in a spendy coat or winter boots for your child, use fabric tape to put her name and phone number inside. It's also worth labeling other favorite items—such as books, dolls, action figures, and beach toys—that might be taken elsewhere and forgotten.

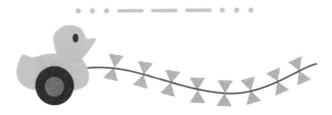

**220** Teach your child the value of money from a very early age. A piggy bank or "helping jar" (where you offer coins for help with age-appropriate chores, such as setting or clearing the table or for getting through bedtime or the morning routine quickly) provides great education for your child—and can save *you* money. Next time your child whines for a treat or a toy, let her know how much it costs and tell her you'll help her count her money when you get home. Having to use her own coins often diffuses desire pretty quickly—and if it doesn't, the item becomes a goal to work toward rather than a given.

• • • ▬▬ ▬▬ ▬▬ • • •

**221** Introduce your children to the concepts of spending, saving, and giving to charity by having three small jars, one for each purpose. Talk about choices of what to buy, what to save for, and what cause they would like to donate to.

• • • ▬▬ ▬▬ ▬▬ • • •

**222** "We'll put it on your birthday list" (or "Christmas list," whichever comes first) is an easy out of buying something on the fly, without your children feeling like they've lost a battle.

• • • ▬▬ ▬▬ ▬▬ • • •

**223** Remember your childhood lemonade stand? Make one. You will be amazed at how much money your child will earn, and what she will choose to do with it.

* * * — — — * * *

**224** Learn to prepare a few simple soups, casseroles, and baked-pasta dishes. Not only do they tend to be cheaper as meals (and freeze well), they are often appealing to small kids, allowing you to feed the whole family for less money *and* less effort.

* * * — — — * * *

**225** Scrounge your office's recycle bin for sheets of paper that are printed on only one side. This is perfect for your toddler's early scribblings or for scrap paper to carry in your tote.

* * * — — — * * *

**226** Damp cloth dishtowels work better on kid's hands and faces than paper towels or napkins—plus they're cheaper, better for the environment, and easy to throw into the laundry you're already doing.

* * * — — — * * *

**227**

"If your toddler has a hard time leaving a toy store empty-handed, tell her the toy/doll/teddy bear lives at the store with his family and cannot come home with you because he would miss them." —*Simone*

**228** Explain to your child what you are going into a store to buy *before* you enter—especially if it's a toy store or other tempting spot. When you're shopping, resist the temptation to buy extra items your child points out that weren't on your list—even if they seem reasonable enough in the moment—because once you open that door, it becomes hard for your child to believe that you are only going to buy X, Y, or Z on future shopping trips.

**229** Let your child accompany you to drop off clothes, books, toys, or canned food to charity. It's the beginning of a long lesson on being thankful for what you have and trying to avoid the "greedies."

- - - ▬▬ ▬▬ ▬▬ - - -

**230** Comparison shop for baby-related items you constantly buy that aren't cheap: diapers, wipes, formula, diaper pail refills, laundry detergent, baby food, etc. When you see you're running low, check online and on two or three store flyers before loading up. It's also wise to save your last receipt for these items so you can determine whether one store's "sale" is a true bargain or not.

- - - ▬▬ ▬▬ ▬▬ - - -

**231** Always buy the largest size of kid staples such as yogurt and applesauce, and divvy it up into smaller containers as needed.

• • • —— —— —— • • •

**232** At restaurants and fast-food chains where "small" drinks can be enormous, order one and ask for two cups to split between children.

• • • —— —— —— • • •

**233** Kids love straws. Buy the reusable hard plastic ones, or cut regular straws in half—it's a better length for small children and you'll get twice as many for the money.

• • • —— —— —— • • •

**234** Save your purchasing dollars for toys that can do multiple duties by inspiring imaginary play, rather than something that can be used only one way. For example, a simple and inexpensive (or used) pop-up tent can be used indoors or out, offer crawling and peek-a-boo fun for babies, a play restaurant or store for toddlers, a fort or dress-up room for preschoolers, and a cozy spot for older kids to go for privacy while reading or doing a craft. (Oh, and you can use it as a tent, too.)

• • • —— —— —— • • •

## 235

"We bought a pack of those colored sponges that are in different shapes—apples, butterflies, stars—at a crafts store. They are supposed to be for sponge painting. But we also use them in the tub, to 'wash' the trikes or wagon in the driveway, to help with hand washing, or to play with out in the garden or the water table." —*Anna*

**236** Hold off on buying new bedding, carpet, or furniture—even if you're dying for it—until your kids are in kindergarten. Besides protecting those big purchases from preschool messes, you'll save for what you really want, earn interest on that money, and avoid having to constantly admonish your kids for jumping on the couch cushions.

**237** Don't be suckered in to those expensive art tables with matching chairs and an art-paper roll built right in, which look so lovely in the upscale kids' catalogs. A piece of butcher paper secured to your coffee table with masking tape works just as well; leave it there as long as you can stand it for doodling (no more coasters!), and switch it to wax paper when it's play dough time. Plus, kids almost never sit to do anything if they can help it, and art is no exception—so special chairs are just something pricey to trip over.

· · · —— —— —— · · ·

**238** To protect your rug during art time, put a splat mat (or one of those plastic mats meant for wheeled office chairs) under your table.

· · · —— —— —— · · ·

**239** Remember that dancing, bubble baths, acting things out, hide-and-seek, and reading or drawing are free and favorite activities for kids of all ages.

· · · —— —— —— · · ·

**240** At mealtime now and then, make things into "samples," just like at the store—with fancy toothpicks if you like. It takes a little more time to chop but a lot less food goes to waste . . . and you'll probably hear a lot less whining, too.

. . . ▬▬ ▬▬ ▬▬ . . .

**241** Avoid overpriced food courts and drive-thrus by always having pb&j or similar sandwiches cut into squares, in case outings run long.

. . . ▬▬ ▬▬ ▬▬ . . .

**242** Buy a good insulated cup for each child that belongs to only him or her. Before any outing that might call for a drink, fill cups with water or juice and ice cubes, and avoid buying drinks out (or packing overpriced juice boxes).

. . . ▬▬ ▬▬ ▬▬ . . .

**243** Juice or yogurt pops are an inexpensive treat you can feel good about. Simply pour juice or yogurt into Popsicle forms, or use ice-cube trays or silicone muffin tins with Popsicle sticks inserted through plastic wrap. This is also a good way to use up some leftover smoothie or the end of a large tub of yogurt taking up space in the fridge.

. . . ▬▬ ▬▬ ▬▬ . . .

**244** Kids happily eat frozen fruit rather than fresh—offering a great chance to use up left-overs rather than throwing them out. When fresh berries are just starting to turn, freeze them to use later on yogurt, cereal, oatmeal, or ice cream. When your child leaves half of a banana or pear on her plate that will only turn brown (and therefore be rejected), peel it, wrap in plastic, and freeze to later use in smoothies or milk shakes.

● ● ● ━━ ━━ ━━ ● ● ●

**245** Keep rewards (and bribes) small. A young child doesn't need to be promised a new toy or an expensive outing for every accomplishment or help with a household task. Kids are thrilled with one Lifesaver, Tic Tac, jelly bean, yogurt-covered raisin, or sticker—especially if that's what they know as a special treat from the beginning.

● ● ● ━━ ━━ ━━ ● ● ●

**246** Every parent of a young child winds up with doubles of lots of stuff, from xylophones to copies of *Goodnight Moon*. Organize a toy/book swap *when your kids are not around* and bring the doubles or toys your child never found interesting. Everyone gets one ticket per item they throw into the pot; the person who brought the most stuff gets to pick first ("paying" for one item with one ticket). This is great to do around holiday time.

**247** If you have even the slightest interest in having another child, save everything you have room for. There is no better money-saver than the ability to grab a plastic bin out of the attic and find a whole new set of clothes, shoes, and diapers as your next child grows. (And really, a baby boy can wear butterfly pajamas.)

• • • ▬▬ ▬▬ ▬▬ • • •

**248** A homemade CD mix of some of your child's favorite songs is a terrific and almost-free birthday present for friends, cousins, classmates, and teachers. Let your child have fun decorating the cover for that personal touch.

• • • ▬▬ ▬▬ ▬▬ • • •

**249** Wait as long as you can before introducing your child to juice, and always mix in extra water from the very beginning so no one knows the difference. Watered-down juice is not only better for your child, it's cheaper for you.

• • • ▬▬ ▬▬ ▬▬ • • •

**250**

"On weekends, we make a huge batch of popcorn (not microwavable) and dole it out in small 'kid-size' portions as a treat that's cheaper and healthier than store-bought snacks. We also add generic soda water ($0.50/bottle) to any juice to make "bubbles"—the kids think it's a big treat, the juice lasts longer, and they never waste any in their glass." —*Brad*

**251** Imaginary play is not only great for your child's budding brain—it's also easy on the wallet. A child who is easily entertained exploring Mom's closet or a whole world under the dining table is not going to whine "I'm bored!" any time there's not an expensive toy or elaborate outing planned. Encourage this play by participating with children until they're old enough to really interact with their peers or play independently. Turn couch cushions into forts or castles, throw a sheet over a table to make a cave or secret grotto, make a simple folding chair a restaurant or ticket booth for the fair. The props you use don't have to be elaborate—or even make sense. Your child will take anything you offer and run with it, if you show him the way.

• • • ━━ ━━ ━━ • • •

**252** Invest a couple bucks in sidewalk chalk, and you can instantly play hopscotch, four square, tic-tac-toe, hangman, and many other games while getting fresh air and watching the world go by.

• • • ━━ ━━ ━━ • • •

**253** Get your child a library card, in addition to your own. Many libraries have no age requirement, and suddenly you can check out more items. Plus, your library may waive late fees on items checked out to children's cards.

• • • ━━ ━━ ━━ • • •

**254**

"There is very little that we do purely to save money, but it seems like when we've made a decision to cut something out or limit it because of simplifying or being more conscious of the stuff we bring into our house, it saves dough." —*Becky*

**255** It's not in everyone's budget to hire a babysitter for regular dates out. Instead, choose one night per week when it's "date night" at home, and take turns planning it. Once the kids are in bed, resist all chores and work—and even all parenting talk. It will all be there tomorrow. Order in from a favorite restaurant, enjoy a movie, dance in the living room, indulge in an elaborate dessert, snuggle, smooch.

# 256. Holiday and Birthday Money-Savers

**Holidays and birthdays tend to be big money drains for young families, and it's hard not to get sucked into the commercialism. Try these ideas to reign in the money while still having fun.**

⚓ Rather than mailing a gift that might not be a perfect fit, ask grandparents or other relatives for a membership to a family-friendly attraction, like the zoo, aquarium, children's museum, or science center. Free outings for the whole family, all year long!

⚓ For your child's first couple of birthdays or holidays, resist buying her gifts. She will get plenty of presents from friends and family and won't know the difference—plus you can save cash for a surprise gift on a rainy day.

⚓ Consider giving your child a present *or* a party, not both—meaning if your child is dying for a pizza or pool party that will cost money, that is his birthday gift from Mom and Dad. Next year, if he's eager for a new bike, he can choose the present option. This makes for a good tradition going forward.

"We bought our Christmas gifts on Etsy.com this year. We spent less, drove less, avoided lines and hassles, plus the creators usually send nice notes and little gifts with purchases. It's community building in its own way." —Becky

 With your circle of friends and family, start a tradition of potluck birthday or holiday celebrations featuring toy/book/game swaps.

 Reign in birthday-party expenses by following the adage that the number of children should match your child's new age (i.e., four kids may be invited to a fourth birthday).

 Remember, no young child cares if his birthday cake is perfect—as long as it's cake, and he's allowed to eat it, he's happy. If you don't want to spring for a store-bought cake, use a simple cake mix (and decorate it together!) for a fraction of the cost.

Enlist your child to make holiday and birthday cards, wrap, and thank-yous. They can also help make banners, signs, and other decor, including decorating regular paper plates with food-safe markers instead of buying fancy ones.

 For warm-weather birthdays, gather at a park or beach instead of a restaurant or other pricey option. Many popular public parks allow you to reserve barbecue pits or picnic shelters for a nominal fee.

 For favors, try one small on-theme gift (such as a soccer figurine, fireman's badge, butterfly barrette, or light-up fairy pen) versus goody bags, which can really add up and proliferate unneeded stuff for guests. If kids will already be doing an activity at the party (decorating wands, T-shirts, or cupcakes), let that be the take-home item.

SANITY-SAVERS

Exactly what counts as a "sanity-saver" when you are a parent? Just about anything that allows you to breathe a little easier, enjoy the day a little more, and remember that you are not alone in this venture. This could be something as simple as figuring out a better way to brush teeth or contain the household clutter, or as far-reaching as asking for help when you need it and carving out some alone time. While the time-savers and money-savers offered in this book might certainly also help your sanity, this section is dedicated to ideas that are purely to help put your mind at rest.

Rest. Oh, that's a nice, if elusive, word. While employing these tips may not give you the chance to sleep until 11 or feel utterly carefree in the way you did before kids, the goal is to find ways to scale back—just a little bit—on the day-to-day things that might be causing you anxiety, frustration, annoyance, or, well, *unrest*. Test out a few gems of sanity-saving advice from other parents who have been precisely where you are, feeling what you're feeling, and looking for solutions. Why not take advantage of their lessons learned? God knows, you deserve it. You have nothing to lose—and a little peace of mind to gain!

**257** Nap when your baby naps. There's a reason it's the oldest parenting advice on the planet.

 **258** Keep your stroller basket stocked with a changing pad or blankie, diaper, and zip-top bag of wipes—plus a few bucks in cash. That way, you don't always have to check, stock, or even lug your diaper bag for short outings.

 **259** It's okay to put the baby in bed with you if it helps the whole family get more sleep.

 **260** Likewise, it's okay to put the baby in his own room from the get-go if it helps the whole family get more sleep.

**261** If you find yourself with too many people stopping by after the baby comes, set visiting hours—like Tuesday mornings and Saturday afternoons—and a time limit. And of course, anyone who wants to meet the baby ought to bring food!

**262** Order every TV series you ever meant to watch via the library or Netflix before the baby comes. If he won't go back to sleep at 3 a.m., you'll be much happier if you're not stuck in front of infomercials.

• • • ▬ ▬ ▬ • • •

**263** If someone offers to hold your baby or entertain your child so that you can eat or shower, take them up on it—fast.

• • • ▬ ▬ ▬ • • •

**264** It's time to lower your standards on home decor. You will only drive yourself crazy if you try to make your home into a child-free magazine image. Instead, save clippings for future ideas—you'll get to them sometime.

• • • — — — • • •

**265** Do your best to avoid comparing yourself to other parents and your baby to other kids. Seriously, there's no point—and it only adds to the anxiety of this already worry-prone stage in your life.

• • • — — — • • •

**266** Get plenty of swaddle blankets and learn to wrap like a pro. Almost every new parent says their baby was happiest when tightly swaddled. If yours always breaks free, try the Velcro variety.

· · · —— —— —— · · ·

**267** Rather than fooling yourself that your post-baby life is the same and saying yes to trips, invitations, and events that might be too stressful, just say no—and don't feel guilty about it. It's okay to turn down plans when you don't have the energy or if something's at a tough time of day for your baby.

· · · —— —— —— · · ·

**268** A top-of-the-line insulated coffee/tea mug is absolutely essential. No one can expect you to stay sane when you have to sip lukewarm or cold coffee for several months straight. It's just cruel.

· · · —— —— —— · · ·

**269** If your child has a "lovey" (a toy or blankie he cannot live without), do yourself a favor and buy a spare one. Keep it hidden in the closet until the inevitable "lost lovey" scenario transpires.

· · · —— —— —— · · ·

**270** As counterintuitive as it is to nudge a sleeping baby, if your baby is not yet sleeping through the night, try this trick to get more of your own shut-eye. If your baby normally falls asleep at 8 p.m. or so and then wakes up at 1 a.m. for a feeding, nudge her awake to eat before *you* go to bed, say at 10 or 11 p.m. That way you're not awakened in just two hours . . . and you might actually get four or five in. Plus, most babies can rouse just enough to nurse or take a bottle on automatic pilot without really waking, especially if you avoid any unnecessary interaction during the feeding.

**271** Avoid houseguests and set-in-stone travel commitments as much as humanly possible. It's stressful enough being a new parent without adding this into the mix.

• • • ━━ ━━ ━━ • • •

**272** Try to wean yourself off the monitor, especially if your baby's room is nearby. Babies make a lot of noises when they sleep and you'll go bonkers if you try to listen to and evaluate each one. It's much better to be rested when they really need you.

• • • ━━ ━━ ━━ • • •

**273** If your baby seems cold-sensitive, put a heating pad or hot-water bottle in the crib when you take her out for night feedings, and remove it when you put her back in. A zip-up sleeping sack (also called a wearable blanket) can also help.

• • • ━━ ━━ ━━ • • •

**274** Remember that you never know until you try. If you've been hesitating about doing some things for yourself—shopping, a manicure, a haircut, lunch with friends—because you're worried about what might happen with your baby in tow, you've got to give it a shot. Young babies sleep a lot, and when awake they're often entertained by new locales, different light fixtures or windows, background music, and friendly faces peeking in to say hello—all of which they will encounter on such an outing.

● ● ● ━━ ━━ ━━ ● ● ●

**275** If you're nervous about leaving your child with someone else (even your partner!), ask for frequent texts, ideally with a picture attached. Seeing a smiling (or sleeping) baby will put you at ease so you can enjoy yourself or focus on your work.

● ● ● ━━ ━━ ━━ ● ● ●

**276** It's okay to go to the movies with a new baby. Hit a weekday matinee and carry your baby in her car seat or baby carrier. She will almost certainly sleep, and if she really melts down, you can always leave.

● ● ● ━━ ━━ ━━ ● ● ●

**277** If you're going through movie withdrawal but aren't sure about a first-run flick with your baby, look in to your city's version of "mommy movies." These are first-run movies offered in the morning to moms with babes-in-arms, usually at a lower price . . . and you're welcome to bring along a friend or partner.

· · · — — — · · ·

**278** Go out to eat at odd hours. Eating Chinese food at 3 p.m. means no one in the restaurant hears your kid fussing and you get great service.

· · · — — — · · ·

**279** Save yourself grooming headaches by trimming bangs, fingernails, and toenails while your kid is asleep. This works especially well in the car seat, when baby is often sacked out *and* strapped in, sitting upright.

· · · — — — · · ·

"My daughter was such a terror about having her nails cut that I used to put on my husband's hiking headlamp to keep my hands free, and sneak into her room at night to do it while she was fast asleep." —*Katie*

**281** Let go of the idea of trying to keep your house quiet. There's no need to stress about doorbells, phones, the TV, guests, or even the vacuum if your baby (who likes ambient noise anyway) gets used to the sounds of the house from the beginning.

**282** Don't ditch your old phone, TV remote control, wallet, camera, or set of keys . . . these will be the best, most distracting toys you ever gave your child. Save them for moments when you really need them.

## 283

"When our kids began to scoot and crawl—but before they could climb up on things—we used ottomans and side chairs to block stairs or hallways we didn't want them in. That gave us some time to decide where we wanted baby gates." —*Lindsay*

**284** Keep a roll of masking or duct tape stocked at home, in your car, and in your bag when you travel. As commando childproofing, it can close a cupboard, cover an electric socket, soften the corners of a sharp hotel table, even keep the tray table closed on a flight. And of course, it can provide quick repairs of all kinds. It can even turn a restaurant napkin into a temporary bib!

**285** When going to a friend's house in the evening, always bring your child's pajamas and a toothbrush in your bag so you can get him ready for bed before heading home. That way you won't have to wake him if he falls asleep on the way home.

• • • ━━ ━━ ━━ • • •

**286** Keep a box in your trunk stocked with a few essentials, including diapers, wipes, a clothing change for you and baby, a blankie or towel, a jacket, sunscreen or a sun hat, a bottle or sippy cup, an extra pacifier (if using), a bottle of water, and some nonperishable food for both of you. One day, probably soon, it will save you.

• • • ━━ ━━ ━━ • • •

## 287

"There's nothing wrong with little white lies that help you out when your kids are young. You can tell them the ice cream truck plays that song when it's *out* of ice cream, or that the race car shopping cart belongs to someone else who brought it from home, or that the TV is asleep for the night. Soon enough, they'll know better." —*Bob*

# Little Lifesaver: Plastic Measuring Cups

*Spend a couple of bucks on your next trip to a super-store and you'll have toys that will entertain your child for years to come. Plastic measuring spoons attached by a ring are a favorite of babies and attach easily to a stroller or car seat. Plastic cups, colanders, and funnels are handy for the bath, sandbox, water or sand table, or playground wood chips. Buy a couple of sets and keep an extra in your car for an unexpected stop at the park or beach.*

Always, always, always have snacks.

 From babyhood through high school, a change of scenery is always good to snap kids out of a snit. Go outside, even just to the front steps, no matter what the weather.

**290** Give yourself permission to "break the rules" sometimes. No matter what your neighbor, mother-in-law, or hot parenting book says is the right thing to do, if you find another way that works better for your family—and it's not endangering your child's safety—go ahead and do it.

## 291

"After trying various alternatives, our baby is so much happier sleeping next to me in only a diaper on his side in our bed—I know it's a total rule breaker, but it's working for us." —*Annie*

**292** Start out calling crackers "cookies" and raisins "candy" so kids think they're getting treats when they're really getting healthy foods. Yogurt tubes popped in the freezer make great "Popsicles" that are healthy, portable, and require no effort to prepare.

## 293

"I turned unused cosmetic bags into 'baby kits.' Each one has a travel-size pack of baby wipes, gauze towel, diaper, disposal bag, diaper ointment, and snacks (cereal puffs, animal crackers, or teething cookies). All my bags have one of these baby kits inside, so that when I get stuck somewhere without the big diaper bag, I am somewhat equipped to handle things." –Aya

**294** If your kid is a picky eater, sneak veggies into familiar foods and save yourself the headache of constantly cajoling her to eat them. Purée butternut squash to fold into muffins or pancakes, cauliflower into mac and cheese, and spinach into berry smoothies. (Also, remember that if your child eats fresh fruit, she's probably getting plenty of vitamins and fiber, so a day without a vegetable won't kill her.)

**295** Serve thicker food to new eaters to improve their success—and your cleanup. Oatmeal, Greek yogurt, hummus, tuna salad, and well-cooked shell pasta are good choices for those trying to master a spoon solo.

**296** Avoid asking your child a question when you mean to make a statement. You can open the door to a debate when there shouldn't be one. Say, "Okay, it's time to get in the car," not "Are you ready to get in the car?" and "Hop on up to the table—it's lunchtime!" instead of "Would you like lunch?" Remember, you are in charge, and something as simple as syntax can reinforce this.

**297** Don't forget how important comfort items are to your child when traveling or simply visiting a new place. Bring her lovey, pacifier, night-light, or special animal or book for these occasions and save yourself a lot of anguish.

## 298

"We used to bring our daughter's pillowcase and top sheet on the road when she was little, otherwise she'd wake up in the middle of the night and freak out that she wasn't home." —*Simone*

**299** Kids' music is fine now and then, but come on. Put your own music into rotation from the get-go, and your whole family will be happier. Your child benefits from a variety of musical styles, and you benefit from not listening to Barney while stuck in traffic. Plus, you never know—you might find that Green Day improves your baby's witching hour more than any lullaby, and your toddler might come to love spinning around the living room to Feist.

**300** Keep a low drawer or cupboard stocked with safe cooking-related items (mixing bowls, salad spinner, wooden spoons, measuring cups) for your toddler to enjoy while you're prepping meals.

* * * ━━ ━━ ━━ * * *

**301** Many new parents get sucked into the unwinnable argument of who is working harder to keep the family going. Avoid falling into this trap! Set up a sensible division of labor with your partner based on your own circumstances, and revisit it often. Be reasonable and fair, and try to see things from your partner's point of view. Bottom line: Even if one person has a hectic full-time job and the other one is the primary caregiver, make sure you are *both* parenting your child—or you risk resentment and disconnection within your young family.

* * * ━━ ━━ ━━ * * *

**302** If your child resists hand washing, a few favorite bath toys that live only next to the sink can help encourage soaping up her hands *and* her "friends" (and might even provide some entertainment for her while you cook or shower).

* * * ━━ ━━ ━━ * * *

**303** Allow your partner—and anyone else who offers to pitch in—to take over and do things their way, rather than trying to do everything yourself. Parenthood is not a competition, and there is no need to be a hero.

• • • ▬▬ ▬▬ ▬▬ • • •

**304** Create a "rainy-day box" that contains a selection of new or not-seen-in-a-while stuff, to bring out when you're cooped up. This is a great place to put recycled toys that no one has played with in a while, odds and ends you've picked up on sale, extra birthday or holiday gifts that you set aside months ago, and a few fresh art supplies such as beads or glitter.

• • • ▬▬ ▬▬ ▬▬ • • •

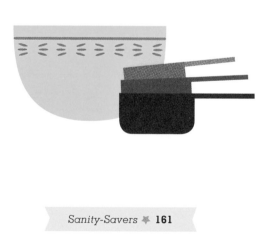

## 305

"Gift wrapping anything is a great activity that your child can do on his own as a 'surprise' for you, while you put your feet up. Just give him some recycled paper, tape, and safety scissors (if ready), and let him wrap anything in sight: a toy, book, the remote control . . ." —*Anna*

**306** If you've come to terms with the idea of candy (and the concept of bribes) for your toddler or preschooler, a bag of Jelly Bellys or Gummi Bears from the bulk-food section—or even a simple box of Tic Tacs—is worth its weight in gold. Hand one out for each current sticky area of your day, like getting shoes on, using the potty, getting into a car seat, or finishing a meal in a timely manner.

## 307

"I use over-the-door shoe caddies with clear pockets for keeping small items—balls, toys, cards, etc.—organized in the kids' rooms. They can easily see what's there and they use a stepstool to reach the higher items."—*Erin*

**308** Let go of the idea that your house is going to be tidy, organized, and clutter-free. Your house has kids in it now. It would be downright weird if it was tidy, organized, and clutter-free.

- - - ▬▬ ▬▬ ▬▬ - - -

**309** When you can manage it, start dinner first thing in the morning while everyone's eating breakfast. It can be a saner enterprise than trying to make it happen at the frazzled end of day . . . plus you have time to remedy a missing ingredient or other roadblock. That night, dinner will be a low-stress snap—just heat and eat.

- - - ▬▬ ▬▬ ▬▬ - - -

**310** Follow the rule that if one thing comes into your house (a new book, toy, dress-up outfit, etc.), something must go. Keep a set number of hangers in your child's closet. When it's time to buy a few new items, it's time to store or donate the same number. This keeps things tidy and streamlined.

**311** When in doubt, throw kids into a bubble bath. It can often fix a sour mood and provide easy rainy-day entertainment for everyone.

**312** Keep to a generally predictable schedule. Young children (and parents) tend to function better if they know what to expect.

**313** If you use a babysitter (and get protests about it), squirrel away a special toy or book, or save a beloved treat, for the days when she appears. It may help dry some tears—and get you out the door—if you tell your child that it's a "Dora Light-Up Doll Night!" or "Pancakes for Dinner Night!" for example, rather than simply a babysitter night. (If your child rides in the sitter's car regularly, a special toy, book, blanket, or cup that lives there is helpful as well.)

● ● ● ━━ ━━ ━━ ● ● ●

**314** Get over your stage fright: Making inanimate objects talk, even in a crowded grocery store or waiting in the airport security line, will save you over and over again. When you sense a meltdown, just have that bottle of detergent do the mambo or have your car keys ask your kid a ridiculous question in a silly voice . . . you'll see.

● ● ● ━━ ━━ ━━ ● ● ●

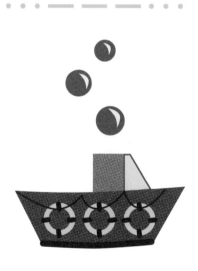

**315** Kids will almost always behave differently (i.e., better) at day care, school, or with a babysitter—and then take out all the day's frustration on their parents. Try to keep it in perspective: Kids push boundaries and unleash their swirling emotions in the place they feel most safe and with the people they know will love them unconditionally. He's not "taking it out on you," he's figuring out what it means to be himself, the good and the bad, in his comfort zone of home.

- - - — — — - - -

**316** Many toddlers love to take pen caps on and off (over and over again), but you might not want her to be wandering around with an open marker. Because Crayola Color Wonder Markers don't mark on anything other than the special paper they're designed for, they're not just for art time—a couple of these can occupy your child in the car, on a plane, in a restaurant, or any place in the house.

- - - — — — - - -

"When our son was around two, he went through a biting phase, which we worried about how to handle. One of our friends had given us a small UglyDoll for his birthday, so we started calling that his 'biting monster,' and any time he felt that he needed or wanted to bite something, he would find his biting monster and bite down on that. He has long since grown out of his biting phase, but whenever he comes across his biting monster in his toys he gives it a good bite, or several."

—*Kate*

# 318. Battles of the Brush

**Hair brushing can make you want to pull your *own* hair out. Here are some ways to make it easier on everyone:**

 Buy a good wide-tooth comb or soft-bristled brush, ideally in a color or design that's attractive to your child (she can even help pick it out).

 Always use a detangling spray on wet or dry hair, and give the spray an appealing name (fairy, princess, dinosaur, or superhero spray).

 For knots and tangles, hold your child's hair away from the scalp and work on the knot from the bottom so that hair isn't being pulled.

 After a hair wash, always detangle and brush while your child is still in the tub and distracted by toys.

 For really challenging hair, consider employing a special song, book, or video that comes out only for brushing time, or a small bribe such as a Tic Tac, jelly bean, penny, or sticker.

## 319

"Trim your child's hair in the tub. They're distracted by toys, and it makes for easy cleanup." —*Mikyla*

**320** If you often eat out in restaurants, a clip-on seat for your baby or toddler can be very handy. Ask for a booth, attach the seat to the table at the inside spot (away from server traffic), and you have a snug, controllable position for feeding your child without the awkwardness of one of those clunky wooden high chairs. It's also much easier than a high chair to take to other people's houses.

**321** Do not get too hung up on the milestones. Everything evens out. If your doctor isn't concerned, you shouldn't be either.

**322** Doctor visits can be traumatic. Try role-playing with your child ahead of time, either with a store-bought doctor set or with something you fashion as a stethoscope or syringe. Use your real doctor's name, look for ladybugs in the ears of stuffed animals, give dolly a shot, and say, "Great job! You were so brave." Be sure to offer a reward—a pretend lollipop for the play visit, and a real one when the time comes.

- - - —— —— —— - - -

**323** There is nothing wrong with earplugs. Use them to take the edge off during super-noisy periods around the house or in the car (when you're a passenger), and to help decompress when your partner has offered you a break to nap, read, or shower.

- - - —— —— —— - - -

**324** Loosen up a bit on clothing choices. You might find you have a smoother day—and a happier child—if you let go of the idea that rain boots, a tutu, and a fire helmet is not an appropriate combination for a three-year-old boy who is going to the playground. Really, who cares?

- - - —— —— —— - - -

**325**

"If clothing is important to you, be sure to dress your babies in cute outfits, because by fourteen months they will wear whatever they want, and I assure you it will not match." —*Jane*

**326** Reverse psychology works shockingly well on most children, no matter how savvy they might seem, beginning at toddlerhood. Tell them, "Whatever you do, don't finish that milk—it's Daddy's favorite!" or "Listen carefully, do *not* put your shoes on yourself! I mean it!" with a mock-serious tone and not only do they do the task lickety-split, they cheer up, too.

"Dare them *not* to do it and they'll do it almost every time. 'Don't eat that broccoli! I'm saving it for me.' Down the hatch it goes. They also love it when I pretend I don't know how to do something—like use a fork or brush my teeth. They take me through every step, laughing as they go." —*Eliza*

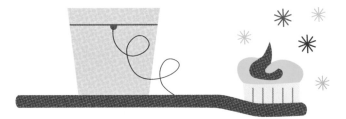

# 328. Toothbrushing Trials

**One of the most consistent toddler battles is toothbrushing. But with a little ingenuity, you can turn it into a game. Try these tips:**

 Name the teeth, whether it's friends from day care, people in your family, or characters from a favorite book or movie. "Open up so I can brush the Ariel tooth! Oh wait, we can't forget Flounder, he's way in the back . . ."

 Give your child the challenge to brush away the "sugar bugs" who are camping/having a party/dancing on their teeth. Go get 'em!

 Sing a favorite song. It's not only distracting, but gives your child a sense of when the brushing will be finished.

 Go on a treasure hunt. Pretend you're searching for a missing fairy, tiger, crown, or whatever will be appealing to your child—and the magic toothbrush is helping.

 Say good-bye to that day's food, naming all the favorite tasty items as you go.

 Pretend you're the dentist and let your child lie back against you, while you "examine" (brush) his very impressive teeth, talking as you go.

 Take turns and have your child brush your teeth, too.

"I sing the ABC song twice in a row when brushing my two-year-old's teeth. It keeps him occupied, gets theABCs brewing in his brain, and is the perfect length of time to hit all of his teeth really well!" —Nicole

"It may be a big money-waster, but I buy my kids new toothbrushes constantly. I try to always find something we haven't had before—a different color, a suction-cup base, or a light-up feature. I think the novelty helps keep them interested. I also finally bought one of those hourglass timers—because I got sick of 'CAN I BE DONE YET?' They are no longer allowed to ask. They can be done when the sand runs out, period."

—Jenna

**329** It's okay to save the bulk of the messy stuff that drives you crazy—from cottage cheese to play dough to finger paints—for preschool, day care, or the patient babysitter.

- - - — — — - - -

**330** If you have a kid who has started refusing to put on her diaper, try this embarrassing but effective technique. Hold up the diaper and speak in a silly voice meant to be that of the character on the diaper (Dora, Diego, Elmo, Mickey Mouse, whatever). Say, "Dora says, 'Molly, please let me be your diaper! I really want to be your diaper! Please come back!'" Watch your toddler come running back so that her "friend" won't be disappointed. (Hey, you might as well make those characters work for you.)

- - - — — — - - -

**331** When your child begins potty training, the previous trick can evolve along with you. "Don't pee on the princesses! They like to stay clean!" or "Spidey says, 'Lucas, I don't want to get wet!'" goes a long way when you're working with training pants or first underpants.

- - - — — — - - -

**332** Magic spells—such as "Bibbity-bobbity-boo, Sarah puts on her shoes!"—can work wonders, because stubborn young kids don't have to feel like they're giving in to what you're asking them to do—it's magic! Inviting them to participate or make up their own rhyme only adds to the potential for success.

* * * ▬ ▬ ▬ * * *

**333** When people are crabby or difficult at the end of the day, stop everything you're trying to do and put a great song on the stereo. Dancing around the living room with your kids beats bickering about dinner anytime—and a five-minute silly break is sometimes all it takes to change the dynamic in your house.

* * * ▬ ▬ ▬ * * *

**334** Give in to a little TV. Your kid's IQ won't plummet from one episode of *The Backyardigans* that makes both of you happy.

• • • ━━ ━━ ━━ • • •

**335** To counteract an upswing in whining or back talk, consider a sticker reward chart or a Nice Voice Jar. Reward your child for a day (or meal) without whining or back talk by placing a sticker on the chart or a coin in the jar. Do this often, especially at challenging points of the day. You can offer a simple reward when your child gets to a certain number, but the motivation is usually seeing the stickers or pennies add up.

• • • ━━ ━━ ━━ • • •

## 336

"Instead of going crazy dealing with all that Halloween candy, I offer to 'buy' a large portion of it from my kids the next day with a toy or a little cash for their piggy bank. As long as they can keep a couple favorites, they are usually happy to hand the rest of it over—and it stops them from constantly asking if they can eat more of it yet." —*Erin*

**337** Take a cue from kindergarten teachers and have your kids help you set some reasonable rules for your home that every family member can follow: things like "We talk to each other nicely" and "We don't push." You'll be surprised with what they come up with. Write them up and have them decorate the sign, then post the rules at kid-level in the kitchen. The pride in helping craft the rules can also help enforce them.

"After a long struggle with toys littering our halls, I put any toy that ended up in the walk-way into time-out. It pretty much trained my son to the point where I only have to pick up the occasional toy." —*Camille*

**339** Encourage primal screams—outside. It relieves stress and can get the crazies out before meals, bedtime, school, or any part of your day when the noise level increases. You might even want to join your kids on this one!

## 340

"I used to go crazy trying to hide the 'Santa gifts' from my kids, because I didn't have much storage space and they were always playing in the closets anyway. Finally I got the brainstorm to hide the gifts inside our luggage." —*Erin*

**341** Let your child be part of the solution when things are going awry. Children as young as two or three years old like to be asked their opinion, and sometimes that input changes everything. For example, if day care drop-off has become a battle, ask how many hugs and kisses he needs to have it be smooth this time. Three? Ten? If he's whining about bedtime, ask him how many minutes he needs to get all the whines out. Four? Six? When he picks a number, agree and stick with it—and praise him for being a problem solver.

"When it's witching hour and my son is starting to be obnoxious, I ask him if it's time to yell at traffic. He gets this mischievous smile and says, 'Yeah!' We both go out on our porch (we live on a busy street) and yell our little hearts out as the rush-hour cars go by—and we both come in feeling much better." —*Lindsay*

**343** Everything is a stage. Don't overthink it, because by the time you begin to get a handle on it, it will be in your rearview mirror. Instead, breathe, commiserate with other trusted parents, and know that this stage will pass . . . and another one will be around the corner.

# Little Lifesaver: Bribes

*Bribes—or "rewards," if you prefer—are part of life as a parent. Think about it, would you follow the rules of your job or strive for a goal offered from higher above without expecting some kind of payment? When thinking about what to use as incentives, remember your kid only knows what he's used to. To encourage good behavior for any challenging part of your day—from potty training to getting out the door for school—choose something that is cheap, simple, portable, and readily available. (And, of course, make sure the item is age-appropriate for your child.) Try single Tic Tacs, Gummi Bears, jelly beans, Skittles, yogurt-covered raisins, stickers, temporary tattoos, plastic "jewels," pennies in a jar. If it works, keep it consistent—don't use different rewards for different actions, or it will get too complicated. Keep a stash of your preferred bribe at all times.*

"When my daughter was having a hard time going to preschool, we invented 'magic school beans'—yogurt-covered raisins, which she'd never had before, in a special pink snack cup. She got these only in the car on the way to school, and it really helped her get going." —ANNA

. . . ▬▬ ▬▬ ▬▬ . . .

"I found a long plastic tube filled with tons of small plastic animals for about five dollars at Target. I dumped these into a velvet bag and used them as 'poopy prizes' for each #2 on the potty. He loved reaching into the bag and being surprised at what reward he got . . . and they only cost pennies apiece." —ELIZA

. . . ▬▬ ▬▬ ▬▬ . . .

"We are currently bribing our nineteen-month-old daughter with ice cream and sprinkles for breakfast if she will sleep through the night. It works, and it's worth it!" —SARAH

**344**

"We have a 'switch' on my six-year-old's back, so that if she's being cranky, we say, 'Oops, forgot to put the NICE switch on.' Then we pretend to switch it and it works 90 percent of the time. It gives her a fresh start without losing face, which is a big deal for the toddler and preschool set." —*Flora*

**345** In your tough moments, remind yourself that despite how it seems, your toddler is probably not having a psychotic break. He is probably just a toddler. He will grow into his brain and his emotions and learn how to handle them. You are not doing anything wrong.

**346** Talk to your partner about what your position is going to be on discipline, time-outs, and consequences for unacceptable behavior. Consistency is the key. Your child needs to know what to expect or she's going to keep testing you to see if she gets a different result.

**347** If you can, have each parent establish a regular one-on-one ritual with each child—for example, Saturday swimming lessons with Dad, or a Sunday evening bike ride with Mom. Not only does one partner get a little break, it's great bonding for the other parent and child to be alone together —especially if that's not the norm.

**348** Set aside your pride and learn to ask for help for both big and small things, when you need it. Ask your friends for dinner at their place, ask your partner for a day off, ask your parents for a house-cleaning service instead of a birthday present. Everyone wants you to succeed.

# 349. Mealtime Mind Games

**Tired of reasoning with your fussy child to finish her meal? Try these tricks:**

 Set a kitchen timer, flip over a board game sand timer, or point to the clock to see if she can get all those peas in her mouth before time's up.

 Tell her that whatever she does, she should absolutely, postively *not* eat that because it's Daddy's (or Mommy's, or Batman's) favorite. Watch her jump at the chance.

 Name the food something that will be more intriguing than the same old thing. "Wow, lucky you! Seven green magic wands!" "You're not brave enough to try monkey brains, are you? You might turn into a monkey! Let's find out!"

 Gossip to someone else (even the dog or a favorite toy) about her eating habits, *in front of her* but not directly to her. "You won't believe this, Mr. Panda, but Mia can eat a whole fish stick! By herself! Well, I'm pretty sure she can . . . I saw her do it before."

Remember the food is always tastier off someone else's plate, so a game of "Who's eating my dinner?" can go a long way with a picky eater. Announce how excited you are to eat, then pretend to nibble on a carrot or other item while you are intent on reading or talking to someone else—with your fork within child's reach. When she takes the bait and you bite an empty fork, be sure to ask what in the world just happened, then repeat.

 New environments are a great way to introduce new foods. When you find a food your child likes at someone else's house and try serving it at home, refer to it as "Henry's Oranges" or "Chloe's Carrots."

 When you have the energy, offering a variety of colors—"Let's eat the whole rainbow!"—cutting or displaying foods in interesting shapes, or putting a "face" on something always helps encourage good eating.

 Bribe them with dessert. It's an oldie but goodie!

**350**

"Don't be afraid to walk out of any place (including restaurants) without having finished what you went in for. It's far less stressful than fighting an unhappy child in a public place! You can always go back to a store later or get your food put into a take-away container." —*Kristen*

**351** Don't let messy or noisy eaters derail ever going out to a restaurant again. Just tip well. They've seen it all before.

**352** Develop a support system of parents you like and trust. They will save you time and again with honest advice, a sympathetic ear, and help with your kids in a pinch.

**353** Get away from it all—even for a few hours. Occasional evenings away from your family are essential for your mental and emotional health. Choose one night every other week that is just for you, and encourage your partner to do the same. Whether you spend it with friends, getting a massage, or by yourself at the movies, you will return refreshed and grateful.

· · · ▬▬ ▬▬ ▬▬ · · ·

**354** Teach your child how to suck through a straw early, and you'll never be stuck without a sippy cup at a restaurant—plus you won't have to clean those annoying valve lids at home.

· · · ▬▬ ▬▬ ▬▬ · · ·

**355** When your child is acting up and you can't figure out why, it's often a need for some one-on-one attention. If you can, stop your day for fifteen minutes and get on the floor to play with your child. Chances are, both you and he will take a deep breath, reconnect, and go forth feeling better.

· · · ▬▬ ▬▬ ▬▬ · · ·

## 356

"When your child is making you furious and you only want to throttle him, tickle him. Laughter is a great diffuser for you both." —*Jennifer*

**357** The end of a fun playdate can be meltdown time. Try to schedule the next get-together right then (even if *you* know it's not set in stone), and your child might be appeased with knowing the good times aren't ending—they're going to be continued very soon.

**358** Leaving notes for your child—even if someone has to read them to her—is a great tradition to start, especially if your child acts out when you leave or travel for work. Set aside a special notebook or pad and leave a simple note on her bed. Encourage her to write back or dictate a reply. As she gets older, this can be a safe place to express fears or communicate things she has a hard time saying aloud.

"One of the things I understand is that when kids hit someone or say hurtful things, they then feel ashamed to say 'I'm sorry,' even if they understand they did something wrong. I give my child the option to 'write' a letter or film a mini video on my cell phone saying, 'I'm sorry, I understand it was wrong to hit you and I love you.' He 'signs' it with his name and a kiss and he feels very proud of himself. He then gives it to the 'sad' person he had offended, and everybody feels very happy afterward. He learns a lesson and also learns how to say I'm sorry with love and without making the issue much bigger." —*Debbie*

**360** Remember, not every situation is a "teachable moment." Often, it helps to delay a talk about a behavior issue or other problem until later on, when tempers have subsided. You'll be more likely to be heard and get results.

● ● ● ━━ ━━ ━━ ● ● ●

**361** Asking your child about "highs and lows" of their day—and offering your own—at dinner or bedtime is a good way to keep connected as a family. No matter how challenging the day, always end it with talking about the good things—very specific moments of happiness, pride, accomplishment, or just plain fun.

● ● ● ━━ ━━ ━━ ● ● ●

**362** You probably know all about time-outs for kids, but don't forget they can also be a useful tool for parents. When your kid is driving you bonkers, take a time-out to calm down or just recharge—even just a few minutes can help immensely. As long as your child is somewhere safe, take a breather by going outside, lying on your bed with a magazine, calling a sympathetic friend, or taking a brisk walk if you've got backup.

● ● ● ━━ ━━ ━━ ● ● ●

**363** A good sweat often does wonders for peace of mind. Finding time to exercise is difficult but not impossible—and it's so important for both health and energy during a physically taxing time in your life. Look in to gyms with child care, a stroller walking or jogging club with other moms, mom-and-me yoga, swapping workout time with your partner or a friend, or exercising at odd times of day, like early morning or late evening when kids are in bed.

**364** Housework can always wait.

· · · ▬ ▬ ▬ · · ·

**365** "Scripts" can be helpful for many kids to prepare for transitions. Practice ahead of time what you are going to say when it's time to leave the park, get in the car for day care, or be dropped off at school. A few funny words in there to shake things up won't hurt ("When it's time for me to walk out the door, let's all yell 'purple pineapple!' instead of 'bye, Mom!'"). When the tough time comes, remind them of what you practiced and ask if they remember their lines. It's showtime!

· · · ▬ ▬ ▬ · · ·

**366**

"Carry food in your purse, always. Your first line of defense should be something like crackers or raisins. If things get really out of hand, you can dole out M&Ms, one at a time. Having a snack or a surprise for bored, hungry, tired kids will save you a lot of tears (theirs) and frustration (yours) when you're waiting in line or riding in the car." —*Lisa*

**367** Parent groups can be a lifesaver. If you don't have a lot of nearby friends with young children, join a new-parent group by contacting your birthing center, hospital, or pediatrician, or by looking online. Some groups even match you by address and birth date of your child. If you hit it off with even one other family, it may be the start of a lifelong friendship for both the adults and the children—and a source of sympathy, advice, and celebration for all the ups and downs to come.

"My kids love to pretend they are us. It is fascinating to see our routines performed before our eyes in high-speed kid play. From Daddy going to work to bedtime tuck-ins, they have it down. It makes me want to slow down and play with them more. It is so easy to get caught up in all sorts of other stuff, but to sit and play for a bit means the world to these kids." —*Simone*

**369** When you're tired of playing drill sergeant, turn things upside down by pretending to be the child. Ask your kids to help you figure out the rules and what should happen next. Children are surprisingly good at explaining the ways things should work in the house, and the empowering change of dynamic can be just what the doctor ordered.

**370** Sunscreen is an important if bothersome fact of life, for you and your child. If you know you'll be logging some sun time later in the day, apply sunscreen on your naked child *before* getting dressed and you'll save the battle at the park when he's trying to run and join his friends. On the go, continuous-spray sunscreen can be much easier to apply in a flash. For little faces, try a sunscreen stick and let your child help apply it himself—and put it on you. Calling it "princess makeup" or a "super-strength invisible face shield" can also help.

· · · ━━ ━━ ━━ · · ·

**371** Communication is key to keeping your mental health intact during the years with young children. Talk to your partner—early and often—about worries, frustrations, and fears, as well as imbalances you see in parenting styles or division of labor. And don't hesitate to seek professional help if the stress of parenthood is affecting you or your relationship in a way that worries you—many counselors and therapists specialize in just this issue, and your doctor should be able to steer you to a good one.

· · · ━━ ━━ ━━ · · ·

# 372. Up with the Roosters

All kids go through stages of early waking (meaning even earlier than the other too-early stages you've lived through). When something prior to 6 a.m. becomes the norm and you want it to change, try these tricks:

 If your child is old enough to know his numbers, put a simple digital clock in his room and cover the minutes with masking tape so only the hour is visible. Teach him that it's okay to get out of bed when the number he sees is a 6 (or a 7, or whatever you think is reasonable). If number sense is still shaky, you can also tape a piece of paper to the clock with the "right" number on it, and tell him to wait for the two numbers to match. All of this can be given an exciting spin by employing any magical creatures or stories that might help get his cooperation. Give lots of reinforcement (or bribes) for success.

 Blackout shades or curtains. Get the good ones. Worth every penny.

If your child comes into your room at those predawn hours and you do not want her in your bed (or she can't be quiet in it), work

"Early to bed, early to rise is really the only surefire cure when you are a mommy. If you're feeling stretched and run down, cut out the caffeine, the sugars, and any other stuff that artificially makes you feel alert for a bit with a mega crash later. Go to bed early, wake up before the rest of the family, and get some exercise and a shower—you will have a new lease on life!" —Simone

together to make a special "nest," "doggy bed," "campsite," "fairy house," or whatever will be appealing on the floor of your room.

 Offer your child a "secret message," such as a kitchen or hall light being turned on, that informs when it's okay to get up. Again, reward his patience.

Every night at bedtime, put a special book, toy, or drawing set next to their bed that is only available to them for those first wake-up minutes. They can play with their "wake-up toy" as long as they like, but once they come into your room, it's put away for tomorrow. You might also decide a no-spill bowl filled with Cheerios, raisins, or crackers—especially if food is not normally allowed in their room— is a good incentive for a few extra minutes of rest.

 Play to their competitive nature: "Bet you can't stay in your room until seven tomorrow!" or "I heard Chloe likes to draw with sparkle markers in her room until seven on the week-ends. Isn't that cool? Would you like to try that?" This can be done in conjunction with any of the other ideas.

If your child is old enough to operate a CD or DVD player, consider allowing her to turn on an audio book or acceptable DVD upon waking (don't forget the headphones!).

**373**

"First of all, I try to think what he is thinking. I understand even though we are both human, we are not the same and we see life from a completely different perspective." —*Debbie*

**374** There's a reason for the backlash against "helicopter parenting." Avoid taxing yourself by being overly attentive to your child during every moment you're together. Remember, parents of multiple children can't hover and dote—and all the kids turn out just fine. Plus, it's *good* for kids to realize early on that they are part of a larger household that needs work, attention, and care to thrive.

**375** Parents invest a lot of undue stress in getting somewhere that's supposed to be fun for their kids. If you don't make it to the aquarium today because your child is happy to poke around at bugs and dandelions right in front of your house, so be it.

• • • ━━ ━━ ━━ • • •

**376** Buy two lunch boxes in August. They can be impossible to find midyear, when your child's lunch box will probably need to be replaced.

• • • ━━ ━━ ━━ • • •

**377** Sometimes you've got to ignore the advice. You will hear or read a lot of parenting advice from the moment you announce your pregnancy until—well, forever. And a lot of it is alarmist, because people love nothing more than telling you what *not* to do. Do not drive yourself up the wall by listening to the Joneses and whatever horror they went through when they tried to go away overnight, give their kid dairy, or let their children share a room. Trust your instincts and rely on the advice of your doctor, and perhaps a couple of reliable parent friends. Ignore any input that doesn't ring true for you.

• • • ━━ ━━ ━━ • • •

**378** Find places you like to spend time that are also enjoyable (or at least acceptable) for your child. You can't spend *all* your time at the playground or toddler music class, after all! Try and you might discover your child does really well at a sculpture park or museum, your favorite French bakery or sushi place, the playroom at your gym, or trolling the shoe department of Nordstrom.

• • • ━━ ━━ ━━ • • •

**379** If your child is ready to give up his nap (but you aren't!), try offering a deal that he *try* to nap for ten minutes and then you'll return to see if he's asleep. If he's not, he can stop trying (and you do have to keep your end of the bargain). When no nap becomes the norm, maintain this time of day as "quiet time," with independent reading, puzzles, or coloring in his room. Consider a reward if he can do this on his own for what you consider a reasonable amount of time.

•  •  •  ━━  ━━  ━━  •  •  •

**380** Evenings can seem so short after the kids are in bed, it's hard to muster up any energy for household tasks. But when you know you have an early morning or important event the next day, take a half hour to set the coffee machine, start the dishwasher, lay out the next day's clothes, set the breakfast table, and pack lunches if needed. You'll guarantee a stress-free jump-start to the day.

•  •  •  ━━  ━━  ━━  •  •  •

**381** Always keep a few extra small toys in the car, in case "sharing day" at school is forgotten. The toys can double as surprise distractions in traffic.

•  •  •  ━━  ━━  ━━  •  •  •

**382**

"Before we moved to London, I created a little book for my daughter. It included pictures of our old and new houses, exciting things that we would see in our new place, and favorite objects and routines that would stay the same. It seemed to really help give her a sense of security and what to expect." —*Siobhan*

**383** Life changes, big and small, are tricky for most young kids. Ask your local librarian or bookseller to recommend books that can help guide conversations about what's coming up for your family— a move, a new sibling, a new school or caregiver, a change of job for a parent. A story can open a lot of doors for children to express how they're feeling—and can open your eyes to what their worries might be.

# 384. Plane Pain

**Remember, the person most stressed about the crying kid on the plane is you—not any of the other passengers. Remind yourself that almost everyone has been in your shoes and most people are understanding. The trip won't last forever, even if it feels like it! Here are some tips to ease the pain:**

⚓ Before a big trip, consider mailing some kid stuff ahead of time. Print out a packing slip online and arrange a free pickup to avoid wrestling all that gear during check-in and at baggage claim. Since you have to pay for luggage anyway, you might even save some money for door-to-door service! Plus, packages are fun to open when you arrive.

⚓ Consider the baggage service and check-in often offered at long-term parking. An extra few bucks per bag might be well worth the hassle of lugging everything yourself.

⚓ The "escort pass" is a well-kept secret that allows your spouse or other adult to accompany you all the way to the gate when you are flying alone with small children. Passes are offered at the airline's discretion, so call in advance for details.

"When going on a plane for extended periods, wrap everything with wrapping paper. This includes snacks, books (some old faves, some new ones), coloring books, crayons, yes, everything. For little ones, it will take them forever to unwrap it, older ones will appreciate the surprise, and some may just play with the tape and wrapping paper." —Simone

 Check with your airline about special food and drink allowances for young children. You can probably bring full bottles or sippy cups as long as you declare them at security. Keep such supplies in a separate large zip-top bag for ease through the line.

 Always check for a family line at security and ask for special treatment if a family line isn't available.

When you get to your seat, cheerfully offer to buy a glass of wine for the person sitting closest to you and your child. Five bucks will buy you a lot of goodwill and diffuse any tension right off the bat.

If traveling with a baby, try to nurse or bottle-feed upon takeoff and landing to help with the change in cabin pressure. Older kids might find relief from a straw cup or lollipop; try anything that promotes swallowing.

If you've got someone still in diapers, make sure to change to a fresh diaper as close as possible to takeoff. (For longer flights, consider a double diaper.) With a preschooler who is newly using the potty, consider an "airplane Pull-Up"—a special one-time-only Pull-Up to avoid dealing with a potty emergency when seatbelts are fastened.

A cramped airplane bathroom is a nearly impossible place to change a diaper. To make things slightly easier, remove as much of baby's clothing as possible at your seat first and, if you've got the gumption, just flip up your armrest, kneel in the aisle, and do the change on a pad on your seat.

"Masking tape is easy entertainment for toddlers on a plane or train. They can tape up the back of the seat, the armrest, and themselves— and it all peels off easily when you leave." —Lissa

 For layovers, check the airport map for play areas that can help pass the time and get some energy out.

 Of course, stock your carry-on bag with never-before-seen snacks, books, and toys, as well as audio books or DVDs with headphones, and a complete change of outfit for your child in case of disaster.

# 385. On the Road Again

Some kids are great in the car. Others aren't. Regardless, a car activity box that your child can reach on his own is a lifesaver. Always refresh the kit with new items before a long drive. When he's old enough, invite your child to help you restock it regularly. Think about including:

- Audio books on CD
- Library books
- Magnetic books, play scenes, or bingo
- A Magna Doodle or Etch A Sketch
- A notepad or workbook and pencils
- A kaleidoscope or play telescope
- Finger puppets
- Action figures or small dolls
- Threading toys (cardboard shapes with holes and strings to thread through)
- A favorite soft toy or blanket
- Mix CDs (where each person in the car gets a chance to pick the next song)

"My friend has a minivan and carries a long pet-store fishnet in the front by her seat. She uses it to pass small items (think a sippy cup or a pack of raisins) to the passenger in the third row of seats at red lights. Saves a lot of headaches." —Simone

Also introduce your child to the joys of looking out the car window. A little nudge, I-Spy style, can help with this. Depending on age and interest, challenge your child to count buses or trucks, to find things that are a certain color or begin with a particular letter, or to shout out when he spots a special letter or number on a billboard or sign (perhaps his age and first letter of his name). You can even keep score and offer a reward when you get to your destination.

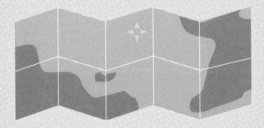

"When our little guy was ten months old (and already moving from walking to running), we went on a road trip that ended up being approximately 1,600 miles. Unlike road trips in our kid-free days, we took away our normal focus on 'getting there.' We used Google Maps on our phones to find little parks in towns we drove through where we could run around and play on playgrounds. When driving through the national parks, we looked for little spots by the side of the road to stretch our legs and have something to eat. We ended up really enjoying our time together and experiencing the amazing scenery in a new way." —Suzie

**386** Meals are not going to be perfect at your house for quite some time. Instead of bending over backward to get all elements of the meal ready and hot at the same time (only to have your child eat the noodles and nothing else), serve it in stages—just like a four-star restaurant! Start with veggies, move on to protein, and offer starch last.

**387** Sharing is hard. Kids can be wiser than their years, and they quickly catch on to the fact that sharing means less of something for themselves. Praise your child for any sharing you witness, and to help avoid struggles, ask her ahead of time what she is willing to share during a playdate or visit. Put away items that are too "special." When tug-of-wars erupt anyway, be prepared to set a timer for turns, come up with a pleasant rule of thumb (such as each child gets it for two songs on the CD), or put the item away temporarily.

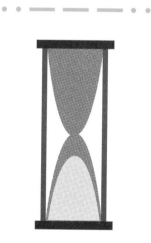

**388** Validating your child's feelings can often diffuse a bad moment. Saying things like, "I know; it's really difficult to leave the pool when you love swimming so much," or "It's frustrating to have to wait for the swings, isn't it?" helps kids believe you are on their side and that their emotions matter.

**389** Ice packs in the shapes of cute critters go a long way in healing bumps and bruises. If kids hear that they're authorized to open the freezer and get out the pink kitty or yellow teddy bear ice pack, they are often quickly soothed or so excited that they forget anything hurts. Ditto for special Band-Aids.

**390** Keep a couple of washcloths that are red or another dark color to use for boo-boos. Kids tend to flip out a lot more if they see spots of blood appear on a light-colored cloth.

**391** Taking medicine—even these days, when much of it tastes like candy—can be a struggle. If it's age-appropriate, let your child administer her own dose (with your supervision, of course) and decide where she wants to be when she takes it—sometimes that element of control is all it takes. You could also try a reward (a spoonful of medicine = a spoonful of ice cream or a Lifesaver) or even shoot the syringe into the straw hole of a juice box and watch it disappear.

**392** Noise, noise, noise! Why are kids' toys all so noisy? Remove batteries of electronic toys that don't have an on-off switch or volume control. You can also cover up the speaker with masking tape to muffle the sound to a more tolerable level.

**393** Art projects can take over your house, beginning in preschool. Instead of trying to save everything, put a few favorites into an accordion file marked with your child's age and create a new folder each year. Other special pieces can be photographed for your digital album or given to grandparents.

**394** Teach your child a couple of very basic card games, such as High Card (what we called War) or Slap Jack (each person flips over a card at the same time, if you see a Jack, slap it and keep it). Carry a deck with you and you have instant entertainment at a restaurant, doctor's office, or airport.

## 395

"If your kids are misbehaving, talk in an exaggerated French accent. It'll annoy the heck out of them, and they'll soon fall in line." —*Lara*

**396** Distraction may be the biggest sanity-saver of all when it comes to young kids. Sometimes just yelling, "Look at that squirrel!" or "What kind of plane is that?" will diffuse crocodile tears. When things get tense, dig deep to find your generous, humorous side, and you'll avoid escalating tempers all around. Make things into a game, speak in a funny voice, sing your request, ask a goofy and totally unrelated question . . . basically, be the bigger person and change your tack rather than digging your heels in.

## 397

"My husband always says, when you're at the end of your rope with your kids, be generous with them. Give more than they might deserve in that moment, and you'll all end up feeling good later." —*Kerry*

**398** Learn to bring the grown-up party to you, when babysitters are too expensive or difficult to coordinate. Put out a few beers and some mixed nuts and invite folks to stop by for happy hour on the weekend. If your kids have a reliable bedtime, invite friends over for a late dinner, dessert, cocktails, or a movie. And please, don't worry if your house is a mess. Nobody cares.

# EPILOGUE: SMOOTH SAILING

Every day as a parent is a foray into uncharted waters; you never know exactly what you're going to get. Just when you think you have something all figured out, surprise! You have to rejigger your perspective yet again. The bonus in all this is that you learn to look at almost everything in a new way. Think about it: Even though parenthood seems to take all your time, your kids will also be your constant reminder to slow down and enjoy the moment. Even though they cost a fortune, they remind you how the most valuable moments in life—tossing a ball in the park, reading under the covers, playing make-believe—are absolutely free. And even though there are times when you feel like you're losing your mind, they have a knack for reminding you that starting a family was the smartest, sanest, best thing you ever did.

I hope the advice in this book helps you navigate some of the highs and lows of daily life with kids, and gives you even more small victories and "aha!" moments to celebrate and share with other parents in your life. May it continue to help you sail a bit more smoothly each and every day. Bon voyage!

# INDEX

# ACKNOWLEDGMENTS

I'd like to offer my sincere thanks to all the moms and dads who took the time to offer their tips, tricks, advice, and insights for this book. You're proof that parents are truly generous folk, ready to help one another get through the rough patches! May you always get back as much help as you give.

Thanks also go to my husband and two beautiful little girls, who provide so much inspiration for what I write, day in and day out.

If you're a reader who has a terrific time-saver, money-saver, or sanity-saver that you didn't see in the book, please share it by visiting www.secondchildfirst.com.